W9-AEQ-385

JOHN G. LAKE
A MAN WITHOUT COMPROMISE

JOHN G. LAKE
A MAN WITHOUT COMPROMISE

by
Wilford H. Reidt

Harrison House
Tulsa, Oklahoma

Unless otherwise indicated, all Scripture quotations are taken from the *King James Version* of the Bible.

Editor's note: All Scripture quotations, including those quoted in material drawn from other sources, have been edited to conform to the Bible version being cited.

7th Printing

John G. Lake —
A Man Without Compromise
ISBN 0-89274-316-6
Copyright © 1989 by Harrison House, Inc.
P. O. Box 35035
Tulsa, Oklahoma 74153

Published by Harrison House, Inc.

Contents

Preface

People have been and are mystified. Why have some individuals been empowered of God? Why have other individuals not been so empowered? How can the difference be accounted for?

There is a unique relationship between the believer and Jesus Christ, the Son of God and Savior of mankind. "I in you, and you in Me" — the relationship is so unique that no single analogy can completely illustrate it. No parable can picture this relationship in its fullness.

The degree to which a believer enjoys this relationship or union with Christ depends on the vision the believer has of the possibilities that are inherent in it. In other words, to fully enjoy this relationship to its ultimate is to know who one is in Christ and to be filled with all the fullness of God.

There is a great potential in this relationship with Christ. The realization of that potential makes the difference. Realization is based on a revelation of the Word of God. One must know in order to achieve. It takes a vision. It takes a revelation. You know who you are in Christ. You know what you are in Christ. You know the privileges of being in Christ. You know the promises are yea and amen. A man who knew all these things was John G. Lake.

It is the object of this study to try to find the secret of his power with God. Does that secret involve one or many factors? What about a man's concept of God? What part does it play in the final analysis?

Acknowledgments

I wish to express my appreciation that the late Gordon Lindsay gave me permission to use material from his books on John G. Lake.

Four of these books are available from Christ For The Nations, P. O. Box 24910, Dallas, Texas 75224. They are: *The John G. Lake Sermons on Dominion Over Demons, Disease and Death; The New John G. Lake Sermons; John G. Lake — Apostle To Africa;* and *Spiritual Hunger, The God-Men And Other Sermons by Dr. John G. Lake.*

PART I

His Early Life

Part I:

His Early Life

His Birth

John G. Lake was born in Saint Mary's, Ontario, Canada, on March 18, 1870. When he was a small boy, he moved with his parents to Sault Sainte Marie, Michigan.

His Conversion

Lake took his first step toward the Lord as a result of attending a Salvation Army meeting. Later, he described the final consummation of that encounter with the Lord: "I made my surrender to Him. The light of heaven broke into my soul, and I arose from my knees a son of God, and I knew it."

While still a young boy, Lake made a decision to live a morally pure life. He wrote: "I never touched whiskey, never used tobacco, never committed an unholy act in the moral sense, but that proud heart of mine had to struggle like a drowning man until I was ready to say, 'Lord, You save me.'"

His Consecration and Healing

"One day while [I was] a young man," he wrote, "God made me aware of my true need when I needed healing from heaven. The disease that had struck my life for nine years and had almost killed me was chronic constipation. I would take three ounces of castor oil at a single dose three times a week. There was nobody to pray for me. I was a member of a Methodist Church, and I had seen God heal one dear soul who was very dear to me.

"As I sat alone I said, 'Lord, I am finished with the world and the flesh, with the doctor, and with the devil; from today I lean on the arm of God.' I committed myself right there and then. There was no evident sign of healing or any other manifestation of God's power, only my consecration to Him; but the disease was gone."

His Success in Business

Lake studied for the ministry in the Methodist Church. In October, 1891, he was appointed pastor of a church in Peshtigo, Wisconsin. However, he decided to go into business instead. He founded a newspaper, *The Harvey Citizen,* in Harvey, Illinois.

In February, 1893, he met and married Miss Jennie Stevens of Newberry, Michigan.

His next move was the setting up of a real estate business in Sault Sainte Marie, Michigan. On the first day of business, he made $2,500. At the end of a year and nine months, he had $100,000 in the bank, $90,000 worth of real estate, and a $30,000 paid-up life insurance policy. During this time he helped found *The Soo Times.*

In 1904 Lake moved to Chicago and bought a seat on the Chicago Board of Trade, no small accomplishment. While there, he handled Jim Hill's Western Canadian land. Jim Hill was the builder of the Great Northern Railroad, now a part of the Burlington Northern system.

While on the Chicago Board of Trade, Lake met some very influential men, successful financiers. Among them were two men by the name of Harriman and Ryan. Ryan employed Lake to form a trust of three large insurance companies, appointing Lake as manager of the trust.

During this period, Lake was already engaged in the ministry. However, he discovered that he preferred talking to a man about salvation to discussing business. He concluded that God was calling him into full-time ministry. But he found it difficult to leave his secular work, because so much depended on him. Finally, he told his partners that he needed a vacation. They responded, "Lake, take a vacation. When you get back, $50,000 a year will look good to you." Shortly thereafter, he left, never to return.

We point out his success in business to emphasize the great sacrifice Lake and his family made in order to follow the leading of the Lord.

In Luke 18:22,23 we read that Jesus demanded one man to give up his material wealth and follow Him. As the young man was very rich, he could not bring himself to do what Jesus asked of him.

However, Jesus treated another rich man, Zaccheus, in a totally different way. He asked nothing of him but a place to abide during His stay in Jericho. Yet Zaccheus of his own accord made the following commitment to Jesus: . . ."Behold, Lord, the half of my goods I give to the poor; and if I have taken any thing from any man by false accusation, I restore him fourfold" (Luke 19:8). In response to his offer, Jesus answered him, ". . .This day is salvation come to this house. . ." (v. 9).

Why did Jesus not make the same demand on Zaccheus that He did on the rich young ruler in Luke 18? Obviously, because the two men differed in their viewpoint of wealth. Money and possessions ruled the life of the young ruler. Zaccheus, on the other hand, ruled over his money and possessions. The reason Jesus made a distinction between these two men is because He knew that nothing must be allowed to stand between a man and God.

John G. Lake understood that principle well. He acted upon it. Feeling that it was what God wanted him to do, he made a drastic move. Whether or not he fit into one of the categories represented by the two men described above, we do not know. Nevertheless, we do know that he decided to dispose of all his possessions and use the money to meet the needs of others.

This was a great sacrifice. Throwing their total trust on the Lord, Lake and his wife agreed that they would disclose their personal needs to no one but the Lord. They would allow Him to supply their needs in His own way. For a while, they went through a period of severe testing. For a time their resources were so limited they could only afford stale bread. However, they stood the test and eventually God's material blessings began to flow in their lives once again.

The question arises, "How much does such a sacrifice count towards the secret of the divine power manifested in the life of John G. Lake?"

To answer that question, let us go back now and consider some of the things which had happened during the time of Lake's successful business ventures.

His Hatred of Disease

John Lake was one of sixteen children. A strange malady infected the children and in time eight of them passed away.

"For 32 years some member of our family was an invalid," he wrote. "During this period our home was never without the shadow of sickness.

"As I think back over my boyhood and young manhood, there comes to mind remembrances like a nightmare: sickness, doctors, nurses, hospitals, hearses, funerals, graveyards, and tombstones; a sorrowing household; a brokenhearted mother and a grief-stricken father, struggling to forget the sorrows of the past in order to assist the living members of the family who needed their love and care."

Perhaps as a result of his own tragic family experiences, throughout his life John Lake hated sickness with a passion.

Again the question arises: "How much did this hatred of disease and sickness contribute to the secret of the divine power manifested in his life?"

His Family's Healing

The conditions in the Lake family at this time were deplorable. One brother had been an invalid for 22 years. A sister of 34 years had developed a five-pronged breast cancer. Another sister was sick with an issue of blood. John Lake's wife, Jennie, was herself an invalid as a result of heart disease and tuberculosis.

It was the message of one godly minister, John Alexander Dowie, which opened the door of hope for the Lake family. They took the brother who had been an invalid for 22 years to the Healing Room in Chicago where Rev. Dowie was ministering.

The brother was instantly healed. Afterwards the sister with cancer was healed. Then, when it looked as though all hope was gone, the sister with the issue of blood was instantly healed.

Encouraged by these miraculous events, John Lake set a time for his wife's healing. At the appointed time, 9:30 a.m. on a certain day, he had everyone he knew to pray. At that precise moment, he laid hands on his wife, and she was instantly healed.

It was during this time of stress that Lake received a great revelation about God's healing power. Allowing his Bible to fall open at random, in Acts 10:38 he read "how God anointed Jesus of Nazareth with the Holy Ghost and with power: who went about doing good and *healing* all that were *oppressed* of the *devil*; for God was with him." Instantly he saw this scripture as the key to the whole Gospel: Jesus is the Healer and Satan is the oppressor.

The revelation is surely one of the keys to the mighty move of the deliverance power of God in the life of John Lake.

His Spiritual
Awakening

PART II:

His Spiritual Awakening

His Sanctification

"Sanctification is calculated to apply to the needs of all our nature, first to the spirit, second to the soul, third to the body," wrote Lake. "Over and over again I have repeated those blessed words of John Welsey in his definition of sanctification. He said, 'Sanctification is possessing the mind of Christ, and all the mind of Christ.'"

When Lake was about twenty years old, a Christian farmer, Melvin Pratt, taught him on the subject of sanctification. Later Lake wrote: "I learned by the Word of God and experienced in my life the sanctifying power of God subduing the soul and cleansing the nature from sin. This inward life cleansing was to me the crowning work of God in my life at that period, and I shall never cease to praise God that He revealed to me the depth by the Holy Ghost of the power of the blood of Jesus.

"A beautiful anointing of the Spirit was on my life," he noted.

"Isn't it marvelous, beautiful, wonderful to realize that mankind can receive into their nature and being the power and Spirit of the Living Christ which contains the purging power to drive forth from the being every particle of evil, every sensuous thing in the thought and nature, so that the man becomes as Jesus is. That is what the blood of Jesus is calculated to do. That is what the Spirit of Christ is purposed to do in the soul of a man — the cleansing of the nature from the power and dominion of sin.

"Beloved, the inflow of Holy Life into our body *must produce* holiness in the *body*, just as it does in the soul. We cannot think beautiful thoughts, we cannot think holy thoughts, without them leaving their impression in our nature, in our very flesh."

To Lake, a holy God must have a holy temple in which to dwell: "And the presence of Christ in the souls of men can only produce first the purity that is in Him. Purity is of God. Purity is the nature of Christ."

Lake believed that sanctification removes that detestable thing that causes sin — the old man, the nature of sin. He emphasized that Jesus came to take away the sin of the world. [1 John 3:8.]

His Hunger for More of God

At this point in John Lake's life, he was assured by many people that he had experienced a beautiful baptism in the Holy Spirit. However, he was not satisfied because what he had experienced had not answered the cry of his heart.

It was George B. Watson of the Christian Missionary Alliance who showed Lake a clearer distinction between the baptism of the Holy Spirit and the experience of sanctification.

A word may be added here. In the early days of the Neo-Pentecostal movement, it was taught that a person had to experience sanctification before he could receive the Holy Spirit.

Later it was discovered that it was possible to receive the Holy Spirit first, before sanctification. However, whether before or after receiving the Holy Spirit, there comes a time when the soul must be subdued and the nature cleansed from that which causes man to sin. All correspondence with sin must be severed.

Lake learned a great lesson from John Alexander Dowie. "Years ago there was no sharper critic of men and methods than I," he confessed, "and on one occasion old John Alexander Dowie taught me one of the best lessons of my life.

"When [I was] subjecting certain of his policies and methods to a sharp criticism, he said [to me], and he exhibited more kindness and more tolerance [with me] than he did with most men who undertook to criticize him, 'When you have had the vision that I have had, when you have shed the tears that I have shed, when you have suffered as I have suffered, when under God you have created a city of 10,000 people, established a body of Christians with an established identity of Christian character worldwide, numbering possibly a hundred thousand, you will be competent to criticize. If you ever develop constructive qualities equal to your critical capacity, you will be a bigger man than I am. At present, however, you are an operator, not a constructor, but you got it in you.'"

John Lake took to heart what he heard and went on to establish a work in South Africa that has lasted for decades. He was a teachable man.

It might be added here that the combined works he started in South Africa number some 700,000 members in a nation of fifteen million.

An aged man walked into John Lake's office one day and revealed to him more of God than he had ever known before in his life. That revelation created a hunger in his heart for what the old man spoke of, the baptism of the Holy Ghost. He had been ministering for almost ten years in the power of God. Hundreds and hundreds had been healed in his ministry. He stated, "I could feel the conscious flow of the Holy Spirit through my soul and my hands."

Still, he was not convinced that he had experienced *all* of God.

His Baptism in the Holy Ghost

"In my youth I took a course in medicine," he recalled. "I never practiced medicine for I abandoned the whole subject a few months before my graduation when it came to the place where diagnosis became the general subject for examination. It was then that I discovered that the whole subject of diagnosis was very largely a matter of guesswork, and it so remains:

"Consequently throughout my life there has remained in me somewhat of the spirit of investigation. It has never been easy [for me] to accept things readily, until my soul [has] stepped out inch by inch and proved them for myself.

"When I approached this matter of the baptism [of the Holy Spirit], I did so with great care, but I approached it as a hungry soul; my heart was hungry for God."

For the next nine months Lake sought for the baptism of the Holy Ghost. He fasted, prayed, and shed tears. Then one day he accompanied another minister to pray for a sick lady. He sat down in a chair to wait until preparations were made so they could pray for her.

Suddenly there fell upon him a shower. It was like a warm tropical rain. It fell upon his innermost being. A great calm came over him and the Lord spoke to him, saying: "I have heard your prayers, I have seen your tears. You are now baptized in the Holy Spirit." Then great currents of power surged through his entire being. He spoke with other tongues.

"For six months following my baptism in the Holy Ghost," he later divulged, "the Lord revealed many things in my life where repentance, confession, and restitution were necessary, yet I had repented unto God long ago.

"Oh, the deep cleansing, the deep revelations of one's own heart by the Holy Ghost. It was indeed as John the Baptist said [of Jesus], "Whose fan is in his hand, and he will thoroughly purge his floor, and gather his wheat into the garner; but he will burn up the chaff with unquenchable fire" [Matthew 3:12].

This cleansing was not the same as the inner healing taught by some. Lake did not go digging into his past. It was only the things revealed by the Holy Spirit that he took care of.

Concerning his baptism in the Holy Ghost, Lake further stated, "And when the phenomena [sic] had passed, the glory of it remained in my soul. I found that my life began to manifest in the varied range of the gifts of the Spirit. And I spoke in tongues by the power of God, and God flowed through me with a new force. Healings were of a more powerful order.

"Oh, God lived in me, God was manifested in me, God spoke through me. And I had a new comprehension of God's will, new discernment of spirit, new revelation of God in me:

"For nine months everything that I looked at framed itself into poetic verse. I could not look at the trees without it framing itself into a glory poem of praise. I preached to audiences of thousands night after night, and day after day. People came from all over the world to study me. They could not understand. Everything I said was a stream of poetry. It flowed from my soul in that form. My spirit became a fountain of poetic truth.

"Then a new wonder was manifested. My nature became so sensitized that I could lay my hands on any man or woman and tell what organ was diseased, and to what extent, and all about it. I tested it. I went to the hospitals where physicians could not diagnose a case, touched a patient and instantly knew the organ that was diseased, its extent and condition and location.

"And [then] one day it passed away. A child gets to playing with a toy, and his joy is so wonderful he sometimes forgets to eat."

We can learn a lesson from this. Lake seems to be warning us against becoming so enamored with the gifts and manifestations of the Spirit of God that we neglect to nourish ourselves regularly from His Word.

Again quoting Lake: "Will you speak in tongues when you are baptized in the Holy Ghost? Yes, you will."

To Lake, baptism in the Holy Ghost meant an outpouring of the Spirit of God upon the life of an individual sufficient to give that Spirit such absolute control of the person that the Spirit will be able to speak through him or her in unknown tongues. To him, any lesser degree of infilling could not be called the baptism (or submersion) in the Holy Ghost. Anything less than total immersion, he would say, and it could not properly be spoken of as an anointing. The person might be "covered" with deep anointings of the Holy Ghost, yet not in sufficient degree to be properly called the baptism in the Holy Spirit.

Not only did the baptism of the Holy Ghost fulfill a deep searching of the heart of John Lake, it also filled him with a great love for his fellow man. Again I quote: "A love for mankind such as I had never comprehended took possession of my life. Yea, a soul yearning to see men saved, so deep, at times heart rending, until in anguish of soul I was compelled to abandon my [secular] business and turn all my attention to bringing men to the feet of Jesus."

"You will speak in tongues," he assured those seeking the baptism of the Spirit. "You will speak with the heart of the Son of God. Your heart will beat with heavenly desire to bless the world, because it is the pulse of Jesus that is throbbing in your soul. And I do not believe there will be a bit of inclination in your heart to turn around to another child of God and say, 'You are not in my class. I am baptized with the Holy Ghost.' That is as foreign to the Spirit of God as night is free from the day.

"Beloved, if you are baptized in the Holy Ghost, there will be a tenderness in your soul so deep that you will never crush the aspiration of another by a single suggestion, but your soul will throb and beat and pulse in love, and your heart will be under that one to lift it up to God and push it out as far into the glory as your faith can send it.

"I want to talk with the utmost frankness," he would tell his followers, "and say to you, that tongues have been to me the making of my ministry. It is that peculiar communication with God when God reveals to my soul the truth I utter to you day by day in the ministry. But that time of communication with me is mostly at night. Many a time I climb out of bed, take my pencil and pad, and jot down the beautiful things of God, the wonderful things of God, that He talks out in my spirit and reveals to my heart."

John Lake was a student of the Word. He never sat down without his Bible handy.

His Vision

"Experimentally I knew God as Savior from sin, I knew the power of the Christ within my own heart to keep me above the power of temptation and to help me live a godly life," he declared, "but when I say to you that when I knew the purpose of God and the greatness of His salvation, life became for me a grand new thing.

"When by the study of His Word and the revelation of His Spirit, it became a fact in my soul that God's purpose was no less in me than it was in the Lord Jesus, and is no less in you and I as younger brethren than it was in Jesus Christ, our elder brother, then bless God, I saw the purpose that God had in mind for the human race. I saw the greatness of Jesus' desire. That desire was so intense that it caused Him as King of Glory to lay down all that glory possessed for Him, and come to earth to be born as a man, to join hands with our humanity, and by His grace, lift us in consciousness and life to the same level that He Himself enjoyed. [When I saw that,] Christ became a new factor in my soul.

"Such a vision of His purpose thrilled my being that I could understand then how it was that Jesus, as He approached man and his needs, began at the very bottom, called mankind to Him, and by His loving touch and the power of His Spirit through His Word, destroyed the sickness and sin that bound them and set them free in both body and soul, lifted them into union and communication with Himself and God the Father.

"Yes, by the Holy Spirit indwelling the souls of men, Christ purposed to bestow on mankind the very conditions of His own life and being, and to give to man through the gifts of the Spirit and the Gift of the Spirit, the same blessed ministry to the world that He Himself had enjoyed and exercised.

"The vision that has called for the shouts of praise from the souls of men in all ages is the same vision that stirs your heart and mine today. It is the vision of the divine reality of the salvation of Jesus Christ by which the greatness of God's purpose in Him is revealed to mankind by the Spirit of the living One, transformed and lifted and unified with the living Christ through the Holy Ghost, so that all the parts and energies and functions of the nature of Jesus Christ are revealed through man, unto the salvation of the world.

"Years ago my legs grew out of shape and my body [became] distorted by the common curse of rheumatism. My pastor said, 'Brother, you are glorifying God,' and my church said, 'Brother, be patient and endure it. Let the sweetness of the Lord possess your soul.' And I was good enough to believe it for a long time, until one day I discovered that it was not the will of God at all, but the will of the dirty, crooked-legged devil that wanted to make me like himself.

"And then, everything was changed and I laid down everything and went to Chicago to the only place where I knew then that a man could get healed. I went to John Alexander Dowie's Divine Healing Home at 12th and Michigan Streets. An old grey-haired man came and laid his hands on me and the power of God went through my being and made my legs straight, and I went out and walked on the street like a Christian.

"Do you know when my legs straightened out it taught me the beginning of one of the deepest lessons that ever came to my life. It taught me that God did not appreciate a man with crooked legs, any more than He does with a crooked soul. I saw the abundant power of the Gospel of salvation, and that it was placed at the disposal of man to remove the unChristlikeness of his life, and if there was unChristlikeness in the body, we could get rid of the curse by coming to God and being made whole.

"For there is just as much unChristlikeness in men's bodies as in men's souls. That which is in the inner life will also be revealed in the outer life. That which is a fact in the mental and psychological [realm] will become a fact in the physical [realm] also. The divine fact of all facts is that the spirit of man and the Spirit of God are of one substance and one nature, and his [man's] mind and body take on the spiritual power imparted, until it, too, becomes Christlike.

"The vision of God's relation to man and man's relation to God is changing the character of Christianity from a groveling something, weeping and wailing its way to tears, to the kingly recognition of the real fact that the Word of God so vividly portrayed in the lesson I read. That ". . . it became him, . . . in bringing many sons unto glory. . ., not one son unto glory, but in bringing many sons unto glory, . . . to make the captain of their salvation perfect through sufferings" [Hebrews 2:10].

"I am glad that the Scriptures have dignified us with that marvelous title of 'sons of God.' I am glad there is such a relation as a 'Son of God,' and that by His grace the cleansed soul, cleansed by the precious blood of Jesus Christ, filled and energized by His own Kingly Spirit, (that he too) by the grace of God has become God's king, God's gentleman in deed and in truth."

John Lake taught a standard of holiness that was not one whit less than what Jesus set forth in His own earthly life. He stood for holiness of spirit, soul, and body. Holiness is one of the keys to moving in the power of God.

His View of Satan

"When the Lord Jesus Christ is born indeed in the soul of man, when by the grace and power of the Son of God, you and I yield ourselves to God until our nature becomes the possessor of that spirit that is in Christ," wrote Lake, "then we begin to realize the spirit of mastery that Jesus possessed when He said: "I am he that liveth, and was dead; and, behold, I am alive for evermore, Amen; and have the keys of hell and of death" [Revelation 1:18].

"That is the reason I do not spend much time in talking about the devil. The Lord took care of him. He [Jesus] has the keys of hell and death, and He has mastered that individual and that condition once and for all.

"If you and I had as much faith to believe it as we have to believe the Lord Jesus Christ is our Saviour, we would have mighty little trouble with the devil or his power while we walk through this world. It is not worthwhile talking about a man after he is whipped out. It is a hard thing for the Christian mind to conceive that the power of the devil is really a vanquished power. It is the triumph of what you know in your own soul. The victory of the Christ and the victory of a soul is in the knowledge of the relationship between your soul and the soul of Christ.

"He into whose heart there comes the Spirit of the living God, has within himself the consciousness of One Who has overcome and Who is set down at the right hand of God, triumphant over every power of sickness and death and hell.

"*Beloved*," concluded John Lake, "*the triumph of the gospel is enough to make any man the wildest kind of an enthusiastic optimist.*"

His Nature
and Lifestyle

Part III:

His Nature and Lifestyle

His Compassion

"Jesus' example on the Cross is set forever as the very acme, and the very soul of the compassion of God," wrote Lake. "After they had pierced His hand, and pierced His feet, . . .with His last breath He prayed to God: 'Father, forgive them; for they know not what they do. . .' [Luke 23:34]; when a man is able to look upon his own murderers, and speak such words as these, surely it shows that he speaks beyond that which the human heart is capable of giving, and is speaking only that which the soul of God can give.

"How long should we endure? How long should we endure the misunderstandings of friends without [giving] rebuff? If we consider these things, surely we see the secret of the life He endured all the way. And unto the very end, and also in the very end, He was blessed of God. His triumph was there.

"The ignorant crucify you, and trample over the loveliest things of your soul, like they bruised the soul of Jesus. The triumph is there.

"Compassion reaches further than law; further than demands of judges. Compassion reaches to the heart of life, to the secret of our being. The compassion of Jesus was the divine secret that made Him lovable.

"Religious people are exacting; good people are exacting; but good folks have to learn to exercise compassion just like others do. Men have loved to have compassion on the lovable, and on the beautiful; but Jesus taught the world to have compassion on the unholy, the sinful and the ignorant."

John G. Lake was a man of compassion. In his entire ministry he never refused a cry for help. He never turned away or refused to answer the call of one who was sick. It made no difference the hour of the day or night.

At one time in Africa he was so tired that he decided to go to a strange city where he could get some rest. It was no time until someone had discovered he was there. Then the people came, the sick, the crippled, the blind. His compassion went out to them. God gave him strength for that time of need.

Mrs. Lake had to learn to adjust to many situations. Once she sent her husband to the store for some groceries. He met a widow lady with hungry children. They got the groceries. When he came home, Mrs. Lake asked about the groceries and he told her what he had done.

Mrs. Lake was a versatile woman. She never knew when he might bring home company and she would have to make things stretch for everyone. Yet she knew that for all his concern for others, her husband had a deep love and regard for his family. They never went hungry.

John Lake had a big heart. One day he caught a young man trying to steal his car. He asked the young fellow why he wanted it. The young man said he wanted to take his girl for a ride. Lake told him that he would not be needing the car until a certain hour of the day and if the fellow would have it back by that time, he could use it. The young man gave his word, and Lake handed him the keys. True to his word, the young man had the car back on time.

His Boldness

"When I went to South Africa years ago," he wrote, "I attended a great missionary conference a short time after I was there. It was a general conference of the Christian missions of the country. On account of our teaching the baptism of the Holy Ghost and the power of God to heal, we were a peculiar feature in the conference. We were bringing a new message and they wanted to hear us, and get us sized up and classified.

"Among the difficulties they discussed in that conference was the tremendous influence of the native medicine men over the people. They called them witch doctors. I talked to the conference about this matter. I said, 'It is a strange thing to me that in all the years of missions in this land, that your hands are tied on account of witch doctors. Why don't you cast the devil out of these fellows and get the people delivered from their power?'

"They took a long breath and said, 'Cast the devil out? He will cast the devil out of you.'

"The secret of our work, the reason God gave us one hundred thousand people, the reason we have twelve hundred native preachers in our work in Africa, is because we believed the promise of: '. . . greater is he that is in you, than he that is in the world' [1 John 4:4].

"We not only went to seek them, but challenged them separately and unitedly, and by the power of God delivered the people from their power, and when they were delivered, the people appreciated their deliverance from the slavery in which they had been held through their superstitions, psychological and spirit control. They are most terrible.

"Once I was called to come and pray for a blacksmith at Johannesburg, South Africa. He was in delirium tremens. When I got to the house they had locked him in a room with the windows barred. The wife said, 'Mr. Lake, you are not going into that room?'

"I said, 'Yes, I would like to.'

" 'But, Brother, you do not understand. My sons are all more powerful than you are, and four of them tried to overpower him and could not do it. He nearly killed them.'

"I said, 'Dear Sister, I have the secret of power that I believe matches this case: ". . . greater is he that is in you, than he that is in the world" [1 John 4:4]. Sister, you just give me the key, and go about your work, and do not be troubled.'

"I unlocked the door, slipped into the room, and turned the key again, and put the key in my pocket. The man was reclining in a crouch like a lion ready to spring. I never heard lips blaspheme as his did. He cursed by every expression I ever heard, and worse. He threatened me [that] he would tear me limb from limb and throw me out the window. He was as big as two of me. I never saw such an arm in my life.

"I began to talk to him. I had the confidence that '. . . greater is he that is in you, than he that is in the world.' I engaged him in conversation until the Holy Ghost in me got hold of that devil, or legion, as the case might be. I approached the bed, step by step, sometimes only three inches, and in a half hour I got up close enough where I could reach his hand. He was still reclining in a posture like a lion. I caught his hands and turned his wrists. I was not practicing any athletic tricks. I unconsciously turned his wrists over, and as I did, it brought my eyes down near his, and all at once I woke up.

"I could see the devil in that man begin to crawl. He was trying to get away. God Almighty can look out of your eye, and every devil that was ever in hell could not look in the eyes of Jesus without crawling. The lightnings of God were there.

"My spirit awoke, and I could see the devil was in terror and was crawling and trying to get back away from my eyes as far as he could. I looked up to heaven and called on God to cast that devil out, and lent Jesus Christ all the force of my nature, and all the power of my spirit, and all the power of my mind, and all the power of my body.

"God had me from the crown of my head to the soles of my feet. The lightnings of God went through me and the next thing I knew, he [the man] collapsed in a heap and flopped down like a big fish. Then he turned out of the bed on his knees and began to weep and pray, because he had become human again, and the devil was gone.

"God anoints your soul. God anoints your life. God comes to dwell in your person. God comes to make you as a master. That is the purpose of His indwelling in a Christian. The real child of God was to be a master over every. . .power of darkness in the world. It was to be subject to Him. He is to be God's representative in the world. The Holy Ghost in the Christian was to be as powerful as the Holy Ghost was in the Christ.

"Indeed, Jesus' words go to such an extreme that, '. . .greater works than these shall he [who believes] do. . .' [John 14:12]. Fear of the devil is nonsense. Fear of demons is foolish. The Spirit of God anointing the Christian heart makes the soul impregnable to the power of darkness."

In the tabernacle in Johannesburg, the platform was so high that a stairway was the only way to get up on it. One night a group of rough Jewish boys wanted to get up on the platform among the girls who were in the choir and orchestra. Lake saw the boys coming toward the platform and knew what it could mean. He called for one of his ushers to help him. In the meantime, up came the boys.

Lake grabbed the first one by the neck and seat of the pants and pitched him through a window just above his head. Then the next one came. He, too, was pitched through the window, and then another. Then the rest got the message and left. The boys dropped from the window down to the ground and went their ways.

It was the power of the Holy Spirit that made this possible. No man could do that on his own strength. It took boldness to meet this situation. It takes boldness to step out and take God at His word. John Lake was a bold man when it came to proclaiming the whole counsel of God.

There is another area where boldness should be manifested in the believer. "Let us therefore come boldly unto the throne of grace. . ." [Hebrews 4:16]. I quote John G. Lake as he spoke at the end of a meeting.

"For years I hunted for this thing I have given you tonight," he told his audience. "That sense of unfitness and unworthiness {or as they call it in psychology, that inferiority complex} swamped me. But when I saw that God became my righteousness, I said, 'I want you to know, Satan, that you have lost your case.' I know what I am now.

" 'For he [God] hath made him [Christ] to be sin for us, who knew no sin; that we might be made the righteousness of God in him' {2 Corinthians 5:21}.

"You, by the new birth, have become the righteousness of God, and God has become your righteousness. God could not make it any stronger than that.

"I say to you reverently, friends, that if you have accepted Jesus Christ and are born again, you are standing in the presence of the great eternal Father God as Jesus is. You have just as much right to step into. . .God Almighty's presence as Jesus has. Don't you see what that means? It means that Satan cannot stand before you any more than he can stand before Jesus.

"Not only that, Jesus gave you the legal right to use His name. And the first thing He tells you to do is to cast out demons. When He gave the great commission, He said, '. . .In my name shall they cast out devils. . .' {Mark 16:17}."

One of the requests John Lake brought to God was to be granted power to cast out demons and release the insane. One day God spoke to him while he was fasting. He was shaving at the moment. God told him that from then on he would cast out devils. From that time on, people came from all over the world for deliverance and were set free. Lake had no fear of any devil or demon.

A lady on crutches came for prayer. She had been to the best doctors in Johannesburg. At that time, she was being treated by a hypnotist.

"Where is the man now?" Lake asked.

"He is there in the front," the woman replied.

Lake stepped forward on the platform and thundered, "You hypnotic devil, come out of him," and after a time added, "and never enter into him anymore."

The hypnotist escaped from the meeting as soon as possible. God perfectly healed the woman.

Later the hypnotist came back and offered Lake a large sum of money if he would give him back his power to hypnotize, as it was his living.

Lake told him, "Man, I did not take it away. God took it from you. Thank Him that you are rid of it. You will never hypnotize another man as long as you live, so go and earn an honest living."

In spite of this, many believed Lake was a hypnotist. One night an enraged mob came into the meeting with weapons, including pick handles. They were declaring what they were going to do to the "hypnotist."

The service continued as though nothing was wrong. At the end of the meeting, Lake walked toward the mob, held out his hand and said, "God bless you." He walked through the mob and not one of them could lift a hand against him.

In South Africa, Lake's name was on everyone's lips. One day a horse was mortally injured in an accident and was lying on the street bleeding to death. Someone saw Lake passing by and shouted, "Why doesn't this man do something for the animal?"

To Lake this was a challenge. So he walked up, removed his hat, and signaled for silence. He kneeled down, put his hand on the spot where the blood was pouring out, and said, "In the name of the Lord Jesus Christ." He left and a moment later the bleeding stopped and the horse stood to his feet ready to go.

Elias Letwaba came into the meeting one day. He was later to be the one to take over when Lake returned to America. Lake put his arm around this black man and called him, "My brother." The unconverted whites in the audience were furious about it. . . .They booed and hissed about it.

Lake turned like a flash and shouted, "My friends, God has made of one blood all nations of men. [Acts 17:26.] If you do not want to acknowledge them as your brothers, then you'll have the mortification of going away into eternal woe, while you see many of these black folk going to eternal bliss. 'Whosoever hateth his brother is a murderer: and ye know that no murderer hath eternal life abiding in him' [1 John 3:15]."

Then Lake held out his hand and welcomed Letwaba. Many in the crowd were for putting the "black devils" out and kicking them into the street. They were shouting it. However, Lake, with his hand still on Letwaba's shoulder, said calmly, "If you turn out these men, then you must turn me out too, for I will stand by my black brethren."

Such love was new to the black man and it won his heart. By the end of the meeting, the gainsayers had fallen into a sullen silence.

Men have been martyred because they were bold enough to stand by that which was right. Lake had made a consecration to preach and teach the highest and holiest things God's Spirit would reveal to his heart, whether anyone would believe it or not. Like Paul, he would stand by the truth regardless of the consequences, even if it meant prison or death.

His Living by Faith

Few people understand the meaning of living by faith. In Lake's meetings no collections were taken. It is strange to realize that during this time, with thousands being saved and healed, the missionary party was often in dire need.

One day Lake returned home to be informed by his son, Horace, that he had given the last of the food to the children for supper and there was nothing for breakfast the next day. Lake said, "Let us pray." Before breakfast the next morning, a vehicle came to the door with food for them.

One day a lady called Mrs. Lake aside and gave her ten shillings, apologizing that the amount was so small. "Small," Mrs. Lake remarked. "Why, even a tickey [a three-penny bit] would be welcome." At the time, the Lake family did not have a cent in the house.

Sometimes they only had corn meal mush to eat. Yet they never grumbled or complained. They also never went hungry. The Lakes made it their policy to make their needs known only to the Lord and to let Him supply according to His riches. To them, God has promised to meet all of our needs, but not all our wants.

Lake put it this way: "It is almost a joke to hear people in America talk of trusting God for their existence while in His service in a land where every man's pocket has money in it. But in a native country, where there is no money, it is different, quite a different proposition."

The people in South Africa believed that the Lake party had money coming from some society in the United States in sufficient quantities to care for their needs. The truth is, the Lakes had gone to Africa without anyone backing them. Another thing that made the natives feel that the Lakes had money was the fact that they rented halls in which to hold meetings. Later, the family did receive some support from Christians in America, but it was not that much.

John G. Lake had this to say about financial support for missions: "I never asked a man for a cent in my life, and I have lived and been able to minister every day. God has met me every time, and I believe He will meet every other man or woman who will likewise put their trust in God and go forward."

Paul admonished Timothy: "Thou therefore endure hardness, as a good soldier of Jesus Christ" [2 Timothy 2:3]. These people of God knew what that meant. But they did not dwell on the hardships. They rejoiced in the mighty move of God in their lives.

Peter put it well when he wrote: "But rejoice, inasmuch as ye are partakers of Christ's sufferings. . ." [1 Peter 4:13]. There was no self-pity manifested in the lives of these men and women of God. Like the apostles, they rejoiced that they were counted worthy to suffer for His name. [Acts 5:41.] They were a happy people.

It appears that the person who is going to go places and do things for God, as was done in the Early Church, must be willing to lay his life on the line for God, even if it means martyrdom.

His Refusal To Compromise

Here was a man who received the Word of God, and no amount of persuasion could turn him from it. Possibly the best explanation of his uncompromising attitude is summed up in his own words. In writing to the leaders of the work he founded in South Africa, he wrote:

"You, brethren, have got a chance to do something. You have got the chance to take up the second step of the work, the molding, and solidifying and systemizing, etc. There are two things essential that in your endeavor to unify you don't slobber [indulge in mawkish sentimentality]. There is a possibility of harmonized cooperation without losing the identity of the thing created.

"But I tell you, if the Apostolic Faith Mission[1] is going to lose her character, her progressiveness, and aggressiveness, and her staunch standing by the original principles and the original doctrines in order to get everybody to work in harmony, my own expression would be, the devil take the harmony.

"There is a unity that only tends to weakness. The necessity of unifying is many times imaginary, especially if one is forced off your original basis."

In a letter to Frank Dugmore in Johannesburg, Lake summed up his meaning in these terse words: "If I were to give you a watchword, it would be 'No compromise,' fight or no fight, discussion or no discussion. Principle is better than unity, and the ultimate end of principle will be oneness."

His Humility

". . .and be clothed with humility. . ." [1 Peter 5:5]. Paul stated that he had served God ". . .with all humility of mind. . ."

---

[1]The Apostolic Faith Mission founded by John G. Lake is not a part of the Apostolic Faith Church of the United States.

[Acts 20:19]. Peter urged the believers of his day: "Humble yourselves therefore under the mighty hand of God, that he may exalt you in due time" [1 Peter 5:6].

Writing of Moses' life, Lake said: "In all history, no man had so many reasons to get puffed up, if he was puffable. The little fellow gets puffed up, the big fellow puffs down."

On another occasion, he wrote: "I always felt, brother, as concerning my life in Africa and my labor for God there, that I was somewhat in the position of which David declares of Moses, when he said [of God], "He made known his ways unto Moses, his acts unto the children of Israel" [Psalm 103:7]. The people of Africa seemed to behold the phenomena of what God did, but God took my spirit behind the scenes and let me see how God did them.

"Another thing, I was a very undeveloped man in many ways. A tremendous baptism of the Spirit had come from heaven upon my soul. At Pretoria, God anointed me in such power as I question of any other man in the history of this movement has ever enjoyed, in so far as we know. The Spirit of God ran through my person like a river of heavenly fluid. Cancers withered under my touch, cripples of every type were instantly restored, works of creation in the bodies of men took place.

"But my soul was not big enough to carry the wonder of God, neither my heart subdued enough. It was an anointing of power. I was compelled to exercise every power of command of my nature to control myself, so that nothing abnormal would take place."

John Lake humbled himself under the mighty hand of God. Yet he testified to the fact that to have God move through him in that degree was itself a humbling experience, as you know it is His love which is doing the works. Humbling oneself under the mighty hand of God is taking the same stance that Jesus took when He said, ". . .The Son can do nothing of himself, but what he seeth the Father do. . ." [John 5:19], and, "I can of my own self do nothing. . ." [v. 30].

The inner development finally came and Lake testified that it would have been easier to have handled the power he had in Africa if this development in humility had taken place there.

His Prayer Life

John G. Lake was a man of prayer. He not only spent time on his knees, but one of his favorite ways of communing with God was by walking and praying. He testified that some of his greatest victories came this way.

Near the end of his life, Lake noticed that his vision was fading. He could not see things clearly and realized that he was going blind. So he took a walk and went into prayer. In the course of his prayer, he told God that it would be a shame for him to lose his sight after all the great spiritual manifestations which had been experienced in his life. God heard him. Just a short walk around the block, and the victory was his. His sight was restored and remained so for the rest of his life.

Later he wrote: "May we say that it is only after the Lord baptized us in the Holy Ghost that we really learned how to pray. . .when He prayed through us — when the soul cries, born out of the Holy Ghost, rolled out of our being and up to the throne of God, and the answer came back — His prayer, His heart yearning, His cry. May God put it in every heart that we may indeed see the answer to the Lord's prayer, 'Thy kingdom come. Thy will be done, in earth, as it is in heaven' [Matthew 6:10]."

As we have noted, for a long time Lake prayed for power to cast out demons. One day God spoke to him that from that day on he would cast out devils. As a result, the insane and devil-possessed were brought to him from far and near, and they were delivered.

Some say that you should never seek the gifts but the Giver, then you will get the gifts. But if you have sought the Giver and He dwells in you, I see nothing wrong with asking Him for the gifts He has for you. We are to desire spiritual gifts. [1 Corinthians 14:1.]

When one sees men and women involved in such a flourishing ministry as John Lake's, the question arises, "When do they find time to be alone with God and pray?"

In answer, Lake stated: "But as the consciousness of the Lord's near return is upon us, one is disposed to press matters, and to work rather than to pray. How glad I am that God has taught me to pray as I run and run as I pray."

Once the anointing that breaks the yoke is upon a person, then to further pray for it is senseless. The anointing is given for service. Go out and use it, and let it use you to destroy the works of the devil. Then you can run as you pray, and pray as you run. The scripture, "Pray without ceasing" [1 Thessalonians 5:17], will take on a new meaning. As you work, your life will be a continuous prayer. Yes, you will need to get alone with God at times.

Perseverance in prayer was one of the things that characterized the life of John Lake. He believed in sticking with things until victory came. I will give one of the more extreme examples from his ministry.

"I want to give you this for your own help and blessing," he wrote. "I knew a man in South Africa who was an ardent Methodist. He had ten sons, all (local) Methodist preachers; and three daughters; three beautiful daughters; holy women; a wonderful family; one of the most wonderful families I have ever known.

"The old gentleman had been stricken with disease, and the agony of his suffering was so great, there seemed to be only one way [to find relief]; and that was to drug him into insensibility. As the years passed, he became a morphine fiend. He told me he smoked 24 cigars daily, drank two quarts of whiskey, and used a tremendous amount of morphine every day. Think of it.

"So the old man, until he was 73 years old, was drugged into senselessness most of the time. I prayed for him unceasingly for 16 hours without result. William Duggin, one of my ministers, hearing of the situation, came to my assistance; . . . I remember how he stood over him and prayed for him in the power of God.

"Somehow there was no answer. I watched that man in convulsions, until his daughters begged me to just let them give him morphine, and let him die senseless, rather than see him suffer longer. And I said, 'No, I have had your pledge and his, too, that life or death, we were going to fight this battle through.'

"Presently, as I stood there, and was watching the awful convulsions, particularly in his old bare feet that were sticking out at the bottom of the bed, this [verse] came to my mind: ". . . Himself took our infirmities. . ." [Matthew 8:17]. And I reached out and got hold of them [his feet], and held them as in a grip of iron; and that thing, that is too deep for any form of expression we know, broke forth in my soul: and in a single moment I saw him lie still, healed of God.

"Many a day after that I have walked with him over his three vast estates, on which were 50,000 orange trees and 50,000 lemon trees, and the old man told me of his love for God, and I had my reward."

Perseverance in prayer paid off. Too many times people give up at the crucial moment.

Jesus ministered twice to a man before he was healed. [Mark 8:23-25.] So John Lake would pray as many times as necessary to bring deliverance to a hurting person, whether the problem was physical or spiritual.

To Lake, the power to pray through to victory was not something to be received and treated as a matter of course. It often meant sleepless nights and battling with the hosts of unbelief. But Jesus wielded this power, and the servants who have carried on His work ever since have needed the same. Lake had known the need of nights of prayer, and wherever men have been willing to deny themselves their nights of sleep that they might abandon themselves to prayer, revival has followed. God is looking for intercessors.

Jesus said, ". . . He that believeth on me, the works that I do shall he do also; and greater works than these shall he do; because I go unto my Father" [John 14:12]. "For he whom God hath sent speaketh the words of God: for God giveth not the Spirit by measure unto him" [John 3:34]. God does not expect us to carry on the ministry of Jesus with less equipment than He had. We need to set our sights high and refuse the traditions of men who say that it is impossible to do as Jesus instructed us.

In a vision, Lake saw an angel take him through the book of Acts, speaking to him these words: "This is Pentecost as God gave it through the heart of Jesus. Strive for this. Contend for this. Teach the people to pray for this. For this, and this alone, will meet the necessity of the human heart, and this alone will have power to overcome the forces of darkness."

As the angel departed, he said: "Pray, pray, pray. Teach the people to pray. Prayer and prayer alone, much prayer, persistent prayer, is the door of entrance into the heart of God."

His Preaching and Teaching

I had the privilege of sitting under the teaching ministry of my father-in-law for about three years. He was an excellent teacher. He had the remarkable ability to create faith in the hearts of those who heard him. He taught six nights a week. I seldom missed a session. He was a student of the Word of God. He had an all-round message and understanding of the Word. He taught not only on healing, but on every other subject necessary to build a good, balanced Christian life.

John Lake never sat down but that he had his Bible either in his hand or within reach. His wife had to learn to sleep with the light on, as he studied so much at night. He always kept a pencil and writing pad handy. Many times he would wake up in the wee hours of the morning and take down the things the Holy Spirit revealed to him. This is the way most of his sermons where given to him.

I remember him saying that one time as he sat in his big chair, God gave him five sermons. He wrote down the notes for all of them. When he asked what to preach on the next Sunday morning, God told him to preach the first message he had received.

His sermons, when I sat under his ministry, were about 20 to 30 minutes long. He would take a point and develop it with living and real illustrations. His sermons were driving, fearless messages. He preached hard. Yet when he ministered to the sick, it was with a marvelous compassion and tenderness. He preached total trust. When a man preaches total trust, and lives by it, his words have the ring of authority.

Lake would say, "Throw your medicine in the toilet, and then apologize to the toilet."

He did not believe in a rigid worship program. He was flexible so that the Holy Spirit could govern the meeting. If ministry to the sick was to come first, that was the way it was done. Either way, it was in accord with the example set by Jesus. When He sent out the twelve, He commanded them to preach and then heal the sick. When He sent out the seventy, He commanded them to heal the sick first and then preach. [Luke 9, 10.]

A baby crying in the audience never disturbed Lake. I remember one time when a baby began to cry during a service. The mother was greatly disturbed. Lake called down from the pulpit and told her not to let the baby's crying bother her. He said that he could preach louder than the baby could cry. Besides, he assured her, the baby would develop a good set of lungs and make a good preacher one day.

One time in Africa two men brought their dogs into the back of the meeting. The dogs got into a fight and soon their owners joined them. Up in front, Lake was going right on praying for the sick and crippled, and they were being healed. Nothing disturbed him when he was doing the work of the Lord.

His Family Life

John Lake had a deep love for his family. One of the greatest blows that ever struck him was the loss of his wife in South Africa. It happened while he was out on the mission field. Suddenly, he felt that something was wrong at home. Before he could get there, Mrs. Lake died. He called her loss "the master stroke of Satan."

The cause of her death is not clear. In South Africa at that time, people took an afternoon siesta of about two hours or more. I heard one of Lake's daughters remark that her mother never took time for a siesta. The daughter felt that this practice contributed to her mother's death.

There is no doubt but that Mrs. Lake would have been delivered had her husband arrived in time. She had been through a very difficult time once before.

In August 1900, she was accidentally shot. The bullet entered near her spine at the waist line and passed through her body, lodging against the skin of her abdomen. I will quote from her testimony as given in the *Leaves of Healing*, June 15, 1901:

"At my husband's home none but Zion people were allowed to come in, and oh, how glad I was to be away from every unbeliever.

"After a while, the pain started in my bowels and ran right through my body up to my shoulders. The suffering was terrible.

"Even those around me did not realize how terrible my suffering was, for the Holy Spirit seemed to go through me all the time giving me power to endure the pain.

"At midnight the pain stopped and I had a sinking spell.

"For a time I seemed to be on the very threshold of the other shore.

"My husband sat by, fanning me and whispered loving promises from God's Word, and soon I was asleep and slept quietly until morning.

"That was the last of my suffering, but I was unable to move from my left side.

"We sent another request to Zion to pray that I might receive strength.

"About the time for prayer I asked my husband to turn me over on my right side, and to pray that I might be able to rest in that position. He did so, and I fell asleep.

"While sleeping, I had the most beautiful dream.

"I appeared to be walking in some of the heavenliest places, and came at last to a high mountain.

"It just seemed as if I were going to enter heaven when the thought came to me, 'Oh, I would rather be healed now and stay with my children.'

"A Voice answered me saying, 'This is the Holy Hill of Zion, and you are healed.'

"I awakened with the feeling of an electric shock going through my body, and found I could turn from side to side freely and without pain.

"From that time I began to sit up a little each day, improving rapidly.

"A week later Elder Bryant came.

"As he examined the wound he said, 'Well, the bullet was swift, but God's healing power was quicker than the bullet.'

"Just two weeks from the day I was shot, I was perfectly well."

Lake's son, Otto, was healed of typhoid fever. Writing about this incident, Lake recalled: "In 1913 I was in Chicago in a big meeting, when I received a telegram from the hospital in Detroit, saying, 'Your son Otto is sick with typhoid fever. If you want to see him, come.'

"I rushed for a train, and when I arrived, I found him in a ward. I told the man in charge I would like a private ward for him, so I could get a chance to pray for him. Well, God smote that thing in five minutes. I stayed with him for a couple of days until he was up and walking around.

"He went along for four or five weeks, and one day to my surprise I got another telegram, telling me he had a relapse of typhoid. So I went back. This time there was no sunburst of God like the first time. Everything was as cold as steel, and my, I was so conscious of the power of the devil.

"I could not pray audibly, but I sat down by his bed and shut my teeth, and I said in my soul, 'Now, Mr. Devil, go to it. You kill him if you can.' And I sat there five days and nights. He did not get healing the second time instantly. It was healing by process — because of the fact my soul took hold on God; I sat with my teeth shut, and I never left his bedside until it was done.

"You may be healed like a sunburst of God today and tomorrow. The next week or month when you want healing, you may have to take it on the slow process. The action of God is not always the same, because the conditions are not always the same."

One time another of Lake's sons came home from school with a note saying that he could not come back until his tonsils had been removed. Lake called him over to himself and prayed. He sent him back to school the next day. The nurse was pleased that the boy had had his tonsils out.

John Lake had faith to meet all the needs of his family.

One might be led to think that his home was a very serious, possibly gloomy place, considering his seriousness about the Kingdom of God. But it was not so. John Lake was a strong, rugged character with a loving and winning personality. He was a man about six feet to six feet two inches tall, and weighed about 200 pounds. He had clear gray eyes and graying hair when I knew him. He had a hearty laugh.

"He was a great entertainer," remembers one of his children. "There was company every Sunday and holiday, and he kept the table conversation light with much laughter. At the table he would request, 'Please pass the butter plate,' or, 'Please pass the cream pitcher.' He said he could not tell a lie, for the butter plate had margarine in it and the cream pitcher had milk in it.

"During the Depression, our meat diet consisted almost entirely of mutton — mutton chops, mutton stew, or mutton roast. It was not an expensive meat in those days. Mother always cooked the roast on Saturday, so by Sunday it did not have the first degree of tenderness. Sometimes Dad would take a chunk on his fork, hold it up to his ear, and have a conversation with it. The reply from the piece of meat was usually that it had come from Noah's Ark.

"One of his favorite sayings was, 'Blessed is the man who tooteth his own horn. For if he tooteth not his own horn, his horn shall not be tooted.'

"One of his favorite stories was of the man who fell into the quicksand. Someone called for help to get him out. A reluctant man, who did not want to get involved, inquired, 'How deep is he in?' The concerned rescuer replied, 'Up to his ankles.' Whereupon the other one asked, 'If he's only in up to his ankles, why doesn't he get out by himself?' The rescuer answered, 'Because he is in headfirst.'

"He loved to tell the story or fable regarding a king of England who had attended a royal symphonic concert. At the end of the program the director asked the king how he liked the program. 'Fine, fine,' replied the king, 'but there was one selection I enjoyed more than all the others.'

"The orchestra agreed to play that part again, but the king could not describe the aria. They played snatches of this and that, but each time the king indicated that it was not the one. Finally they played the whole concert over, but the king could not recognize his favorite. Then the orchestra took time out to tune their instruments, and the king cried out, 'That's the one! That's the one!'

"He loved to read Will Roger's newspaper column and appreciated his wry sense of humor."

Lake could laugh at anything, and he appreciated the American society who could find humor even in tragic circumstances.

One day Lake prepared to go on a trip. His wife was suddenly burdened and tried to talk him out of going. He took one of his sons along. After he left, Mrs. Lake went into the bedroom and entered into intercessory prayer.

Sure enough, Lake was involved in an accident. His boy was running about seeking his father and crying out, "Dad, where are you?"

His dad was under the car. Now those old cars were built high enough off the ground that you could crawl under them. Lake asked the boy, "Can't you see anything of me?"

"Your feet are sticking out from under the car," his son answered.

"Well," replied Lake, "just start at my feet and follow up, and you will find my body, and my head is on the other end."

Fortunately, no one was hurt.

One book Lake enjoyed and which was good for many a laugh was Daniel W. Streeter's, *Denatured Africa.* Streeter was a very humorous writer. The book is a story of him and his son on a safari in Africa.

"Some of Dad's favorite hymns," his daughter recalls, "were 'Majestic Sweetness Sits Enthroned,' 'Oh Thou, In Whose Presence My Soul Takes Delight,' 'Crown Him, Crown Him!' ('Look, ye saints, the sight is glorious, see the Man of Sorrows now!'), and 'Arise, My soul, Arise.'

"He loved symphonic and opera music. The Ford Sunday Evening Hour was one of his favorite radio programs. He loved the singing of the Scottish tenor, Harry Lauder, and sometimes sang Lauder's song, 'The End of the Road.' Other favorites were the tenor, Caruso, and the violinist, Fritz Kreisler. His older children gave him a beautiful Edison phonograph on his 50th birthday, and we had many lovely records, as well as a few humorous ones such as 'K-K-K-Katy.'

"Dad regarded all saints as kings and priests before God and desired us to treat them as such," his daughter says. "He had a very great consciousness of being a king and priest before God, and his bearing and demeanor was always that of nobility.

"I can almost see him wrinkle his nose and twist his mouth over the lower concept born in some old songs such as 'such a worm as I,' for he felt that low concept was a disgrace to the blood of Jesus and the purity of the Holy Spirit who raised us to 'sit . . . in heavenly places' [Ephesians 2:6]."

Neither Lake nor his wife ever discussed different members or adherents of the church, or those he went to minister to in their homes. There was never a disparaging word about anyone allowed, no gossip, not even opinions about other brethren in the Lord.

"He believed and trusted everyone implicitly, even to his own damage," his daughter testifies, "for he felt they had to prove themselves in integrity or lack of it. He kept all counseling confidential, and we never knew whom he was visiting. He felt everything given to him in confidence must remain that way, between him and the confessor, even though the person was guilty enough to be apprehended by the law.

"He was generous to a fault. He felt a great obligation to care for the poor, and often we were poorer than those he gave to. On many occasions he gave our meager household allowance to others, and Mother had to adjust as best she could. He would veritably give the shirt off his back. He became known as a 'soft touch,' but in this too, he would rather give to the unworthy rather than shut his soul against them.

"He always had his Bible within arm's reach, and often he and Mother would share scriptures with each other. I recall Mother's excited voice over a verse of scripture that was made real to her. 'Listen to this, John,' or, 'Have you ever noticed this verse, John?' And often Dad would do the same with her. 'Listen to this passage, Florence.'

"In the tabernacle in Spokane, the last place of ministry, he held meetings on Sunday afternoon so that people from other churches could come and be healed and take the blessing back to their own church. He encouraged them to do so. He wanted to see people delivered from the bondage of sickness and take the message to their own churches and start the practice of praying for the sick in them.

"He never turned down a sick call for prayer, day or night. He got up at any hour of the night to minister to the sick, fearful, troubled or even fighting people. He had services six nights a week and twice on Sundays, and made house calls throughout the day and often in the night."

PART IV

His Ministry

Part IV:

His Ministry

His Amazingly Fast Clip

At age fifty-eight, Lake wrote: "I have worked at such an abnormal pace."

Concerning one period in his life after he had received the Holy Spirit, he gave this picture: "Then came as never before the power to preach the Word of God in demonstration of the Spirit. Oh! the burning fiery messages! Oh! the tender, tender, loving messages! Oh! the deep revelations of wondrous truth by the Holy Ghost. Preaching once, twice, sometimes three times a day, practically continuously these four years and four months. Oh! the thousands God has permitted me to lead to the feet of Jesus, and the tens of thousands to whom He has permitted us to preach the Word."

In an area of South Africa known as Potgieter's Rust, a man by the name of Amm owned a farm. Here Lake would go from time to time for a rest. Invariably Letwaba, a national black preacher, would also be called. He would bring the sick and maimed with him. Thus, instead of rest periods, these visits would be turned into times of ministry. It was useless to try to hide the fact that Lake was in the area.

A native woman, very sick with malaria, was brought to him there. Lake, very tired and overworked, was taking a nap in the cool of the farm house veranda. Nevertheless, noting the woman's arrival, he got up and went out to the wagon in which she was lying. There he ministered to her by laying his hands on her head in the name of Jesus Christ.

In a moment the woman jumped up and began laughing and praising God for her healing.

The following is a report entitled "One Day With God in South Africa," written by one of Lake's partners, Tom Hezmalhalch:

"A native over six feel tall, with pain all through his body and deaf in the left ear, was perfectly healed.

"A Dutchman was demon-possessed. He could not stand with feet together without trembling from head to foot. In the name of Jesus, the demons were cast out, and the pain and trembling left. He is happy and well. His wife and two grown sons were healed yesterday.

"Four people came from a distance with a four-mule team. The old man was deaf, but now delivered. The young man healed of diseases of years' standing. The grandchild was healed. The wife came crawling into the room almost helpless, left so after the birth of her son twenty-four years ago. She also had a sprained ankle that was very sore. Imagine her joy and surprise to find no pain while going around the room twisting her body and throwing her arms in every conceivable manner. The three oldest were saved. Praise God, almost every one who comes gets saved.

"A poor couple came, the woman blind and the old man hard of hearing. He was born with weakness and sickness, never knew what it was to be without pain. He was healed, got his hearing, and she her eyesight. They are well known. The people stare to see him walking without his stick, and she without being led.

"A sister came with cancer on her breast and other troubles. The cancer was healed, together with [the other ailments].

"I have just left the Native Hospital after having prayed with twenty-one patients. I wish you could have seen how the Lord healed them. Glory to His name!

"Vryheid, Natal, August 26, 1908."

I heard Lake testify to the fact that one time he was so tired that he went to a distant city for a rest.

However, he was not there but a few hours when he was discovered, and the sick, maimed and crippled came for healing. He talked to the Lord about it, and the Lord asked him, "Where is your faith?" The Spirit of God strengthened him, and he ministered to all who came.

In the midst of Lake's ministry in South Africa, a British publisher who was considered the best in his generation, William T. Stead, sent for him. Stead paid all expenses for the trip. (I might insert here that Mr. Stead later lost his life on the *Titanic.)*

This newspaper man was a spiritualist and wanted to talk with Lake about his activities. It is difficult to get men to see the difference between spiritualism and its seances, and the move of the Holy Spirit of God. (Lake's article on the visit appears at the end of this book. It is entitled "Spiritualism.")

While in England, Lake preached to the combined clergy of the Church of England. They too had sent an investigation party to South Africa to see what was going on. (The sermon Lake preached on this occasion also appears at the end of this book under the title "Triune Salvation.")

Lake also taught for G. Campbell Morgan in his church. He never filled Rev. Morgan's pulpit, as time did not permit. Rev. Morgan said that he did not believe in faith healing, but he did believe in divine healing because he knew a man who prayed for the sick and they were healed. Lake also preached in the church pastored by F. B. Meyer.

On his way back to Africa, Lake stopped at the shrine of Our Lady of Lourdes in France where many thousands of people came seeking healing. Here he put out a challenge to show the real healing power of God. Five hopeless cases were chosen for him to pray for. Three of the five were instantly healed. One was gradually healed, and the fifth one eventually died.

During his entire time in Africa, Lake kept up an abnormal pace because of the tremendous needs he faced there. He later gave the following account of his condition at the time of his departure for home: "When I got on the ship to return to the United States after being in Africa, my eyes turned blind, and I was a tottering wreck. But God pulled me out of that."

He further stated: "When I returned to America, I visited Brother Fockler in Milwaukee, and we talked nearly all night every night for a week. I just wanted to talk and listen. He could talk the thing my heart was longing to hear. Then I came to Chicago, and poor Brother Sinclair was nearly worn out, for I was hungry for fellowship. There was such a passion in my heart to hear his words and assimilate his thought, and to speak out understandingly; such a longing in my soul to hear of the blessing of God, and their point of view.

"So for almost a year we traveled from city to city, as God led, contacting this soul and that soul, until that longing hunger was satisfied, and I felt I could settle down in my own work again."

His Work in the Healing Rooms at Spokane

About 1915, Lake moved his family to Spokane, Washington. He rented a suite of rooms in the old Rookery Building. The Healing Rooms (as they were called) operated under the International Apostolic Congress, Inc., of which John G. Lake was the overseer. The International Apostolic Congress had been formed in London, England. It was moved to Spokane because of the outbreak of World War I.

In 1928, Lake wrote: "In the way of individual miracles of healing, we have as great miracles of healing as there were in Africa in our church here, but not in the numbers.

"We have a woman, Mrs. Teske, who developed a fibroid tumor of thirty pounds — she is a woman of thirty-five. She had been healed under my ministry years ago of other difficulties. But after six or seven years, she developed this tumor.

"Just visualize a thirty-pound fibroid tumor. I do not know whether you have ever seen one. Just imagine a twisted mass of muscle and sinew, arteries and veins, teeth and hair, and you have this tumor.

"Imagine the most disorganized, twisted and jumbled mass that is possible, composed of these constituents, and you have a real fibroid tumor — utter lack of any show of organization. One tooth here, another there, a hair here, another there, and throughout the mass, veins and sinews and muscles twisted, like you would take a bunch of small snakes and twist them into all the shapes you could think of.

"Next get the weight of it. A thirty-pound tumor is equal to three and a half large babies. Twins are usually about seven and a half pounds; it would require four or more such babies to make the weight of this tumor.

"One day in the agony of her soul, when she could not lay down and could not sit down because of the awful compression, she stood up and threw her hands to heaven, and cried out, 'Jesus, heal me now!' The power of God struck her; that mass began to twist and crunch and wither and diminish, and the action was so terrific she cried out, at the top of her voice, 'Oh, Jesus, not that way, not that way.' But in three minutes the thing was totally gone, it had absolutely dematerialized; no blood, no puss, no substance — all had utterly vanished.

"Brother, this is the quality of healing we have, but not the quantity."

In the five years the Healing Rooms were open, 100,000 people were known to have been healed. On May 4, in the *Spokane Daily Chronicle,* was listed an incident from each day of the week:

Sunday, 2:45 P.M. — A suffering woman, insane with an agony of pain, pronounced incurable by her physicians, excepting possibly through operations which were to take place Monday at 9 o'clock. Cause, diseased mastoids. Hands were laid upon her, the power of God flowed into her, in five minutes her pains were gone, to the astonishment of herself and household.

Monday — A group of baffled physicians, a woman dying of spinal meningitis, raving in delerium, their treatment of no avail. Her broken-hearted parents, the prayer of faith, the touch of God, recovered consciousness, the joy of the household, a gathering of friends and relatives to a meeting of praise to God for the healing.

Tuesday — Two men quarreled, a fight followed, a crushed head, a surgical operation, a long period of suffering, the final announcement of the physician, "The man must die." The other man facing the possibility of a trial for manslaughter, his sorrowing wife and children. A telephone call, a quick response, two ministers of the church arrive, hands are laid on the dying man, the power of death smitten, in a few minutes the agony of suffering had disappeared and life had returned. He conversed without pain for an hour and is recovering.

Wednesday — A mother with her little son, three years old, who was strangling with membranous croup, his face black, bronchial tubes refusing to act, the physician could do nothing more; a woman of faith kneels by the bedside, ministers in faith and prayer to the dying child, and in the evening the mother presents the child to her friends well.

Thursday — A long-distance call from a city a hundred miles distant. The father is dying of cancer. The petition is presented to a public meeting at the Healing Rooms, prayer for the dying man is offered by the congregation. Another telephone call two hours later to tell us, "A marvelous change has taken place." Telephone calls each day since. Reports continued — rapid recovery.

Friday — A doctor of medicine, who has suffered from extreme diabetes, and who has spent a hundred thousand dollars in going from institution to institution all over the world where the promise of healing was held out, hearing of the power of God in our midst has been ministered to for some weeks past, came to report his final perfect healing, and that his weight has increased thirty-five pounds, and that he is perfectly well by every known scientific test.

During the years I sat under the ministry of John Lake, he still traveled at a fast clip. He taught six nights a week. He preached twice on Sunday. No matter how tired he was, or what time of the day or night, he would go to the home of distressed parents to minister to a sick child (or any other person who was ill). He hated the devil and all his works. He believed that the quicker you got after the difficulty, the better.

John Lake had a real pastor's heart.

His Manifested Power

And my speech and my preaching was not with enticing words of man's wisdom, but in demonstration of the Spirit and of power:

That your faith should not stand in the wisdom of men, but in the power of God.

1 Corinthians 2:4,5

This was true of the ministry of John Lake from its beginning to the end of his life. For eight to ten years before Lake was baptized in the Holy Spirit, the power of God moved through his life in saving, sanctifying, and healing power.

He prayed for power to cast out devils, as recorded earlier in this writing. God granted his request according to the Word. People were brought from far and near and were delivered.

Following is the testimony of a Mrs. Lakie: "I was violently insane. I was a cook in a lumber camp. My husband and the men in the camp strapped me to the bed with straps. I tore the bed to pieces, injured two of the men so badly they were unable to work for some time. I escaped into the woods and at length fell unconscious in a thicket and lay in the rain for six or eight hours until found.

"The men from the camp brought me in a motor car to Spokane to the court for my committal to the asylum, but on the way the foreman said to the rest of the men, 'My wife was healed in Spokane at Mr. Lake's Divine Healing Rooms after dozens of doctors had pronounced her incurable. Let us take Mrs. Lakie to him before we go to the court. It may be God's will also heal her.'

"So they took me to Mr. Lake's. Mr. Lake and Mr. Fogwill laid their hands on me and in Jesus' name rebuked the demon and cast him out. In one minute I was well.

"Mr. Lake then sent me to Mrs. Benton's to board and I continued to attend the meetings for ten days. A large abscess in my side that had been there fifteen years disappeared in twenty-four hours. I had rheumatics so bad that a bone formation formed between all my toes and forced the joints apart. In forty-eight hours the bone formation was gone.

"During my insanity, a man would appear to me, standing at the foot of my bed, and would say to me, 'Look up, God can heal you.' When I saw Mr. Lake, I recognized him as the one that the Spirit had shown me, although I knew nothing of him, or he of me.

"I thank God for this marvelous salvation. Jesus is ten times dearer to me since I have seen His great salvation for spirit, soul, and body.

"Sunday, July 15, 1917."

When he arrived in South Africa, an anointing fell on Lake that was beyond anything he had imagined. He testified it was like liquid fire running through him.

In one meeting, a man kept getting up and interrupting Lake. Lake pointed his finger at the man and told him to sit down. The man dropped to the floor and lay there for two hours. When asked what happened, the man said it was as if a bullet had gone through him.

John Lake enjoyed greeting people as they came into the meetings. In South Africa, this posed a problem because the power of God was so great upon him that people would fall under it in the doorway when Lake shook hands with them.

There were times when people who came within six feet of him would fall. One thing that concerned Lake about this great anointing which came upon him was the fact that people would fall so violently when he laid hands on them. So to give him peace about it, God told him just to raise his hand about two feet from them. Then Lake was satisfied when they fell. Certainly no one could say he had pushed them over.

Creative miracles were a part of his ministry. An example — Spokane, Washington, August 11, 1914:

"I, Charles Balhiser, herewith certify that I have had eight operations by various physicians for diseased mastoid and ear drums. In the operations, one ear drum and three sections of bone were removed. It left my ear totally dead.

"In the operations, when the left ear drum was removed, the second ear drum was scraped. The doctors then gave up all hope.

"I came to be prayed for. Brother Lake laid his hands on me and asked God for Christ's sake to heal my ears. Today I had a conversation over the phone [using] the [formerly] dead ear and heard perfectly, for which I praise God.

"Signed: Charles Balhiser."

One time during a meeting in South Africa, Lake was sitting on the platform. Another man was preaching. A young Jewish man kept getting up and interrupting the speaker. John Lake arose and told the young man that he would bury him in three days' time. It was a warning.

The young Jew left the service and went to the races. While he was there, in a freak accident a horse kicked through the protective barrier and killed the young man. The Jewish Rabbi refused to bury him, a priest also refused, and so Lake held the funeral.

Had the young man settled down and stayed in the meeting, he would not have been killed. His death was not a judgment of God. The Lord knew in advance what was going to happen and revealed it to Lake.

This is not the time of judgment. Jesus said, "And if any man hear my words, and believe not, I judge him not: for I came not to judge the world, but to save the world" [John 12:47]. When will this young man be judged? Jesus said, ". . . the word that I have spoken, the same shall judge him in the last day" [v. 48].

Wallace, Idaho, 1920:

"Rev. John Lake, Spokane, Washington.

"Dear Sir:

"I became totally blind from glaucoma. My suffering was so intense that Dr. Foster of Denver removed the right eye, but the sight did not return to the other eye.

"Friends recommended me to go to Rev. John G. Lake's Healing Rooms, and my wife took me there, leading me by the hand. I was ministered to three times and my sight was entirely restored, and I am working every day, praising God that I have found that the days of miracles are not past, and that the power of God still flows through the hands of men like Mr. Lake and his associate ministers who give their lives to Him.

"Signed: J. B. Mooney."

Wallace, Idaho, April 28, 1920:

"Rev. John Lake, Spokane, Washington.

"Dear Sir:

"I suffered with weak lungs for over a year, and after my husband's wonderful healing of blindness, I went to Mr. Lake's Healing Rooms and was prayed for once by laying hands on my chest and back. The power of God flowed through me and I was at once relieved.

"Shortly afterward my friends insisted that I must be x-rayed. The photo showed the lungs to be full of spots of bright new tissue and the doctors could not understand it, but I knew, for God had healed me when I was prayed for and the new tissue had grown into the tubercular spots.

"No words of mine could express my gratitude to God for my healing, and we continually delight in telling our friends of how we were healed through God, by His servants at the Healing Rooms.

"Signed: Mrs. J. B. Mooney."

Healing promotes boldness. It was a part of a prayer in the book of Acts that healings, signs and wonders be done, that through these God would grant boldness to His people. [Acts 4:29,30.]

Following is the testimony of Mrs. W. F. Romer: "I was an asthmatic, and had suffered from the disease in its worst form. No words can describe my suffering. The strain of these attacks at last resulted in heart exhaustion and leakage of the heart.

"When I was in one of my terrible spells, when I was propped up in bed, fighting for every breath to live, Mr. Carter told my husband of his wife's healing by the power of God.

"So my husband telephoned to Mr. Lake, asking him to call. As he was too busy, he sent one of his assistant preachers, who prayed for me. I was relieved, but not entirely healed; then I had a relapse and it seemed that my end had come.

"Mr. Fogwill, who was ministering to me, seeing my desire to live, said, 'I am going to try to bring Mr. Lake with me this evening.' That night when I was in the throes of a terrible spasm, Mr. Fogwill and Mr. Lake arrived, laid their holy hands on me and prayed. A soothing calm came over me; as they prayed powerfully, rebuking the asthmatic demon in the name of the Lord.

"Suddenly, something loosed. I could breathe freely; next the clutching and bubbling at my heart ceased, and today I am here, well. How can I tell it? How can I praise God enough?"

During one eighteen-month period, one hundred churches were born out of Lake's tabernacle in Johannesburg. During this time he had what he called a spirit of discernment. Any difficulty that arose in a church, he was shown it before anyone could report on it. A letter or a visit would straighten out the trouble.

One man brought an accusation against a minister that was quite severe. The troublemaker came to see Lake. Before he arrived, Lake discerned that the trouble lay in this man and not in the pastor. So Lake proceeded to show the man his basic problem and get him lined up with the Word.

Another aspect of this ability was the fact that at every meeting, Lake could look over the audience and see all the filth, fornication and vileness in the heart of each sinner. It became quite a burden to him, and he asked the Lord one day to take it away. God responded, but when the ability left, it all went. Later, Lake realized that asking for its removal was not a wise move on his part.

In this section, it might be fitting to repeat something we have mentioned before. I quote Lake: "Then a new wonder was manifested. My nature became so sensitized that I could lay my hands on any man or woman and tell what organ was diseased, and to what extent, and all about it. I tested it. I went to hospitals where physicians could not diagnose a case, touched the patient and instantly I knew the organ that was diseased, its extent, and condition and location.

"And [then] one day it passed away. A child gets to playing with a toy, and his joy is so wonderful he sometimes forgets to eat."

We can learn from these experiences as to how to keep that which God gives us.

Creative miracles were also manifested in Lake's ministry. One day a young lady came to the Healing Rooms sick. The men prayed that God would make her whole. She had had a total hysterectomy. In three months, she returned to the Healing Rooms a little disturbed. She was pregnant. One thing could be counted on for sure. When the staff at the Healing Rooms united in prayer and prayed that a person would be made whole, that is what would happen.

Miss Celia Prentice came to the Healing Rooms in steel braces. She had been born with one leg two inches shorter than the other. After being ministered to, she now walks with both legs equal and her feet are the same size and shape. That was not a healing — that was a work of *creation,* fulfilling the pattern that was in the mind of God, bringing the structural form of that girl to where God saw that "it was good."

There is Mrs. Jenkin's son, whose shoulder was injured in a fall. It became tubercular so that twenty-six sections of rotten bone came out of the shoulder. God healed him and he is taking his place in the world — a whole, healthy, happy, holy man as God intended him and every other man to be.

Some other public testimonies: Mrs. Robert Mott was born blind in the right eye. Her sight was restored as she sat in Hillside

Congregational Church listening to Lake's message on faith in God.

Mrs. Lawrence Bamford had been suffering from appendicitis for months. Because her leg was drawn up, she could not walk. She could not be operated on because of a weak heart. After prayer, she was instantly delivered from pain. The contracted limb came down, she arose and walked, praising God, and has continued well since.

Mr. Robert Mott wore a truss for twenty years to support a rupture. After being ministered to through prayer and the laying on of hands, he took off the truss and continued to do his usual daily work.

One of his sons, Ted, served in the Navy. One time the younger Mott took his father through the battleship. On a panel he showed him a set of keys. When these were pushed, the big guns on the front would rise. Those buttons caused the arms to move right and left. They also fired the guns. This gave the father an idea. The next time he was called to minister to a sick person, he asked God to let him push the right buttons or keys that would release the power of God's healing to that person.

One time Lake had a vision. He was riding a lumber carrier. It was one of those kind that has long legs and the lumber is carried underneath the driver who sits up on top. Whenever Lake tried to go forward the thing would go backward. When he wanted to turn right, it would turn left. He was having an awful time trying to drive it.

Then the scene changed. Lake was standing on the deck of a great ocean liner. It was beautiful, smooth sailing.

Lake asked God the meaning of the dream. He was told that the lumber carrier represented his life when he tried to run it. The ship ride represented his life when he allowed God to run it.

He wrote: "It is our low standard of Christianity that is accountable for much of the shame and the sin and the wickedness of the world. We pattern after Jesus in a sort of way. We imitate Him by doing the things that He did, that is we *outwardly* do them. We perform kind deeds, such as we see that Jesus did.

"But the secret of Christianity is not in doing. The secret is in *being*. It is in being a possessor of the nature of Jesus Christ.

"In other words, it is in being Christ in character, Christ in demonstration, Christ in agency of transmission. When a person gives himself to the Lord and becomes a child of God, a Christian, he is a Christ-man. All that he does and all that he says from that time forth should be the will and the words and the doings of Jesus, just as absolutely, just as entirely as He spoke and did the will of the Father."

It is when we allow the Holy Spirit to take over that the sailing can be smooth in spite of the storm around us. Lake often spoke of the "eye of the hurricane." There is a calm in the eye of the storm.

One of the secrets of power is to abide in the perfect leading of the Holy Spirit.

His Two Secrets

In spite of His great ministry, Jesus had opposition. Among other uncomplimentary things that were said about Him, He was accused of having a devil. Jesus warned His disciples about what His detractors would do to them after He was gone: "For if they do these things in a green tree, what shall be done in the dry?" [Luke 23:31].

Despite the great move of God through John G. Lake, there arose stiff opposition and jealousy in South Africa. Some people were so set against him they wrote letters to the United States accusing him of misusing monies sent to him for the mission work. Though the Lakes went to South Africa with no one backing them, there were those who sent them money. Eventually, the accusation of misusing the money proved to be false.

In the meantime, however, the contributions dwindled to a trickle. It was as a result of this situation that the following incident took place which Lake describes in his own words:

"Do you know why God poured out His Spirit in South Africa like He did nowhere else in the world? There was a reason. This example will illustrate.

"We had one hundred and twenty-five men out on the field at one time. We were a very young institution; were not known in the world. It is ten thousand miles by way of England to the United States [there was no air travel in 1908]. Our finances got so low under the awful attack we were compelled to endure that there came a time I could not even mail to these workers at the end of the month a $10.00 bill. It got so bad I could not send them $2.00. The situation was desperate. What was I to do? Under these circumstances, I did not want to take the responsibility of having men and their families on the frontier without real knowledge of what the conditions were.

"Some of us at headquarters sold our clothes in some cases, sold certain pieces of furniture out of the house, sold anything we could sell to bring those one hundred and twenty-five workers off the field for a conference.

"One night in the progress of the conference, I was invited by a committee to leave the room for a minute or two. The conference wanted to have a word by themselves. So I stepped out to a restaurant for a cup of coffee, and came back.

"When I came in, I found they had rearranged the chairs in an oval, with a little table at the end, and on the table was the bread and wine. Old Father Van der Wall, speaking for the company, said, 'Brother Lake, during your absence, we have come to a conclusion; we have made our decision. We want you to serve the Lord's supper. We are going back to our fields. We are going back if we have to walk back. We are going back if we have to starve. We are going back if our wives die. We are going back if our children die. We are going back if we die ourselves. We have but one request. If we die, we want you to come and bury us.'

"The next year I buried twelve men, sixteen wives and children. In my judgment, there was not one of them, if they had had a few of the things a white man needs to eat, but what they might have lived.

"Friends, when you want to find out why the power of God came down from heaven like it never came down before since the times of the apostles, there is your answer.

"Jesus Christ put the spirit of martyrdom in the ministry. Jesus instituted His ministry with a pledge unto death. When He was with the disciples on the last night, '...he took the cup, ...saying...' [Matthew 26:27a]. Beloved, the *saying* was the significant thing. It was Jesus Christ's pledge to the twelve who

stood with Him, For this is my blood of the new testament. . .'
[v. 28]. Then He said, '. . . Drink ye all of it' [v. 27b].

"Friends, those who were there and drank to that pledge of
Jesus Christ entered into the same covenant and purpose that
He did. That is what all pledges mean. Men have pledged
themselves in the wine cup from time immemorial. Generals have
pledged their armies unto death. It has been a custom in the race.
Jesus Christ sanctified it to the Church forever.

"'. . . my blood of the new testament. . . . Drink ye all of it.' 'Let
us become one' [says Jesus — paraphrased]. 'Let us become one
in our purpose to die for the world. Your blood and Mine together.
'. . . my blood of the new testament. . . .' It is My demand from
you. It is your high privilege.'

"With the exception of John, not one of the disciples died a
natural death, as far as we know.

"That is the kind of consecration that established Pentecost
in South Africa. That is the reason we have a hundred thousand
native [national] Christians in South Africa. That is the reason
we have 1,250 native [national] preachers. That is the reason we
have 350 white churches in South Africa. That is the reason that
today [the time of this writing] we are the most rapid growing
church in South Africa.

"I am not persuading you, dear friends, by holding out a hope
that the way is going to be easy. I am calling you in the name
of Jesus Christ, you dear ones who expect to be ordained to the
Gospel for Jesus Christ tonight, take the route that Jesus took,
the route the apostles took, the route the Early Church took, the
victory route, whether by life or death.

"Historians declare, 'The blood of the martyrs was the seed of the Church.' Beloved, that is the difficulty of our day — we have so little seed. The Church needs more martyr blood."

Many a period in South Africa, the Lake family lived on corn meal mush, and they did not complain. Because they rented halls for meetings, the people thought they had a great source of income, which they did not. At the same time, John Lake was preaching to thousands.

Lake also wrote to two men in this country, "Just a word before the mail closes. Do not let these things [the letters and accusations brought against him which had been sent from Africa] trouble you, and don't worry for us at this end of the battlefield. The work is good, clear and progressive. My soul is strong, my body is strong, . . . my mind is clear, and the devil is on the run. . . .

"I know how my letters sound on the other side of the world, but what do these things count for here, after a meeting like last night's (Sunday), when people were saved and others instantly healed of cancer, rheumatic cripples, etc., right in the presence of five hundred people? I am only sorry for the awful privations some of our workers are enduring because offerings are being largely cut off from the homeland, because of these false accusations.

"But this work is going on, regardless of all that hell can do. It is God's work and men cannot stop it. The work throughout the country never moved more blessedly than in the last six months. Our native [national] work is strong, good, and clear; and it is being extended with marvelous rapidity.

"I feel that we are reaping the result of the prayers of a multitude of precious saints of God whose prayers have gone before, and have followed us night and day. At the Missionary Training Home, Alliance, Ohio, the entire school spent one hundred and twenty days and nights in continuous prayer for missions.

"I have felt from the day my foot touched African soil, I passed into an anointing of God hitherto unknown by me.

"God promised me in a message from heaven the second night I was in Africa, that salvation should flow as a tide, and the healing of our God a mighty river, and verily it is so.

"I have a pile of testimonies of marvelous healings in answer to the prayers of the congregation such as I have never seen before anywhere, in the same period of time.

"In my personal work it has not been my experience, as in former time, to preach conviction for sin upon people by long and hard effort. The Spirit of God has already convicted them. On Thursday last I visited three homes: fourteen persons were converted, and four instantly healed, one of them a woman that had a tumor of twenty pounds.

"Under this new anointing that came upon me as I reached South Africa, I have been enabled to take hold of God with a living faith that I never before possessed in the same degree. We have ceased to ask people before praying for them, whether they are Christians. We have simply accepted the commission as given in Luke 9:1-6 and Mark 11:22-26, and have assumed that when Jesus spoke these words, He spoke them to the disciples and not to the people."

John Lake never blamed the sick if they were not healed. He believed that all the faith required of the sick was that they call for and submit to prayer and the laying on of hands. Then it was the faith of the person or persons praying that saved the sick.

This is in agreement with the word as given in James 5:15: "And the prayer of faith shall save the sick, and the Lord shall raise him up. . . ."

PART V

Conclusion

Part V:

Conclusion

The Key to His Power

The object of this study is to find the key to the flow of the power of God through the life of John G. Lake. Is there any particular thing in his life that is outstanding which might be that key? Really, is there a single key? Let us examine a few ideas:

1. What about his concept of God? He always presented God as a loving, merciful, kind and longsuffering (patient) Father. This concept was based on Jesus' example, as He was the visible image of the invisible God. God's feelings for people were fully expressed through Jesus' ministry and teaching.

John G. Lake fully believed that sickness was of the devil [Acts 10:38.], and that Jesus came to destroy the works of the devil. [1 John 3:8.]

Lake believed that God was a good Father and that His fatherhood should be reflected in those who are fathers in this life. In Deuteronomy 8:5, we find this statement from God Himself: "Thou shalt also consider in thine heart, that, as a man chasteneth his son, so the Lord thy God chasteneth thee."

We ask this question, "What kind of a father is God comparing Himself to in this passage?" Is it a father who brings up his children in the nurture and admonition of the Lord [Ephesians 6:4], or a father who is a child abuser? A good father would never give his son a disease as chastisement. A good father would never want his son broken up in an accident. Neither does God, our wonderful heavenly Father.

Jesus never used abuse to train His disciples for the work ahead of them. Jesus is our life and example. This concept of God as heavenly Father provides a basis for believing that it is God ". . .who healeth all [our] diseases" [Psalm 103:3].

Certainly our concept of God as a Father will be a governing force in our lives. But is it the only key to the flow of God's power?

2. John G. Lake was a man who loved God and His creation. Compassion, an ingredient of love, was outstanding in his ministry. It brought great results.

Jesus' compassion was always followed by a move of mercy. He ". . . saw a great multitude, and was moved with compassion toward them, and he healed their sick" [Matthew 14:14]. ". . . for there went virtue [power] out of him, and healed them all" [Luke 6:19].

If there is going to be any move of the power of God in a person's life, compassion is a key to that power. Is it the only key?

3. In Lake's ministry, holiness was stressed. He had a well-balanced ministry. The Holy Spirit is the Spirit of holiness. "Follow peace with all men, and holiness, without which no man shall see the Lord" [Hebrews 12:14]. (At the end of this book, we have included an article on holiness written by Lake.) A holy God needs a holy vessel to work through.

Holiness is a key to God's move through a life. Is it the only key?

4. John G. Lake was a bold man. He never hesitated to declare the whole counsel of God.

Boldness is a key to the move of God in a man's life. Is it the only key?

5. He was totally consecrated to all the will of God. He made great sacrifices. His consecration was without reservation or compromise.

His son, Livingston (Jack), said of him, "He never let anything stand in the way of his dedication to see and pray for the sick. He never let himself get lazy. I never remember him taking off when he had the sick to care for. Total dedication!"

No doubt a total consecration is the key to the flow of the power of God through a life. Is it the only key?

6. "Where there is no vision, the people perish . . ." [Proverbs 29:18]. Where there is no vision of the healing power of God, the people perish from disease. Where there is no vision of the saving power of God, the people perish in their sins.

John G. Lake had a vision. He had a keen insight into God's will and power. As a result, multitudes were saved from sin and disease.

We can say that a vision is necessary to a successful ministry of any kind. But is a vision alone the key to the move of God through a life?

7. ". . . and be clothed with humility. . ." [1 Peter 5:5]. John G. Lake stated that the flow of God's power was a humbling experience.

No doubt but that humility is a key to the move of God through a life. But is it the only key?

8. John G. Lake was baptized in the Holy Spirit with the evidence of speaking in tongues. As we have mentioned before, he said that tongues was the making of his ministry. Why would

he say this? "He that speaketh in an unknown tongue edifieth himself. . ." [1 Corinthians 14:4]. Edifieth means "builds up." ". . .building up yourselves on your most holy faith, praying in the Holy Ghost" [Jude 20].

Communing with God in tongues is certainly a key. Is it the only key?

9. John G. Lake was a man of faith. He lived by faith. He was called by men a builder of faith. He could inspire faith into the hearts of those who heard him expound the Word of God. When a person lives and practices his faith, it gives power and authority to his teaching of the Word.

The question arises: is faith alone the key to a great move of God through a life? It surely plays a major part.

10. Lake was also a man of prayer. He lived in constant conscious communion with God. He taught that prayer was effective at all times. He won great victories while walking and praying.

Is prayer alone the key to a great move of God in a life?

11. John G. Lake believed that three things contributed in general to a healthy Christian life, though there may be others. These were: 1) a good confession to other people of one's faith, 2) a constant prayer life, and 3) a constant feeding on (reading and studying) the Word of God.

Are these three the only keys?

12. Another aspect must be considered. John G. Lake believed that intercessory prayer was a key to the move of God through a life.

Is intercessory prayer the only key?

Could any one of these dozen aspects which we have considered be called *"the* key" to the power of God?

No, it seems that not one can be ignored. Each plays a part. No doubt but that *all* of the aspects must be present in the person's life if there is to be a great apostolic move of God.

There is one more aspect to consider. What about God's grace? The Apostle Peter urges us: "But grow in grace, and in the knowledge of our Lord and Saviour Jesus Christ. . ." [2 Peter 3:18]. What does it mean to grow (enlarge) in grace? The more you know of God's Word and the more you put it into practice in your life, the more God's favor is extended to you.

It is said of our Lord: "And Jesus increased in wisdom and stature, and in favour with God and man" [Luke 2:52]. He increased (grew) in favor (grace) with God and man.

As you grow in knowledge, you come to understand how to become humble and to remain humble. As you grow in knowledge, you learn how to develop and maintain right motives. As you grow in knowledge of the Word of God, you learn how to give all the glory to God. You learn how to deny self so you will not fall into the snare of the devil and become selfish. You make Jesus Lord of every aspect of your life, without reservations.

God is looking for believers who will ". . .grow up into him [Jesus] in all things. . ." [Ephesians 4:15]. "And to know the love of Christ, which passeth knowledge, that ye might be filled with all the fulness of God" [Ephesians 3:19]. To be filled with the fullness of God means to be filled with the completeness of His being. To the extent one is filled with all the fullness of God, to that extent he will be effective in his work for the Lord.

What does it mean to be filled with all the completeness of His being? Jesus is the image of the invisible God. Being filled with the completeness of God's being is having the character of Christ manifested in you. How can you tell if you are filled with the fullness of God? The fruit of His Spirit will be manifested in your life.

The measure of the fullness of God which you possess is the measure of the grace or favor He can give you. There are blocks to His move. He is looking for a completely surrendered life.

As you grow up in Him (Jesus) in all things, the more trustworthy you become, as you know how to keep your humility.

One thing that is to be avoided is writing something that is going to hinder another's experience in God. For example, one time I read of how a great anointing came on a man because of a great amount of intercessory prayer that was going on (or had been going on) in his behalf.

It was presented as if this was the only reason for his success. If that were so, then I, as an unknown, did not have any hope for much of a move of God in my life, as I did not have a lot of intercession going on for me, even though all the other conditions were present in my life.

This experience raised the question: is the intercession of Jesus alone sufficient to bring about a move of God in a life?

Then I thought of the 120 disciples on the day of Pentecost. No one was interceding for them, except the Lord, though there was intercession for them later on as they continued in the ministry.

As an unknown, you are loved by God. He will see that you get started. Once you have begun, then many others will take you to their heart in intercession.

Another thing you may not be aware of is that God may have already laid intercessory prayer on people's hearts for you.

I would like to conclude with the words of an angel given in a vision to John G. Lake while he was pastoring in Portland, Oregon. In answer to a cry from Lake's heart, the angel took the Bible and opened to the book of Acts. He called attention to the outpouring of the Holy Spirit on the day of Pentecost, and then proceeded through the book pointing out the great, outstanding revelations and phenomena in it. Then the angel spoke these words:

"This is Pentecost as God gave it through the heart of Jesus. *Strive for this. Contend for this. Teach the people to pray for this.* For this, and this alone, will meet the necessity of the human heart, and this alone will have the power to overcome the forces of darkness."

As the angel was departing, he said: "Pray. Pray. Pray. Teach the people to pray. Prayer and prayer alone, much prayer, persistent prayer, is the door of entrance into the heart of God."

His Prophetic
Utterances

Part VI:

His Prophetic Utterances

The Secret of Power

The message below was given in tongues by the Holy Ghost to John G. Lake at 2 a.m., June 18, 1910, in Cookhouse C. C., South Africa.

And, behold, I send the promise of my Father upon you: but tarry ye in the city of Jerusalem, until ye be endued with power from on high.

Luke 24:49

But ye shall receive power, after that the Holy Ghost is come upon you: and ye shall be witnesses unto me both in Jerusalem, and in all Judaea, and in Samaria, and unto the uttermost part of the earth.

Acts 1:8

"He is risen, He is risen! hear the cry
Ringing through the land, and sea, and sky.
'Tis the shout of victory,
Triumph is proclaimed,
Heralds of God announce it,
Death's disdained.

"Shout the tidings! Shout the tidings! Raise the cry,
Christ's victorious, Christ's victories cannot die,

For the bars of death He sundered,
Satan sees that he has blundered,
As the shouts of angels thundered,
"He's alive!"

"Catch the shout, ye earth-born mortals, let it roll,
'Till the echoes o'er the mountains, from the center to the poles,
That the Christ of earth and glory
Death has conquered. Tell the story,
He's the Victor, He's the Victor!
So am I.

"For this reason, that my ransom He has paid,
I've accepted His atonement, on Him laid,
He, the Lamb of God that suffered all for me,
Bore my sins, my grief, my sickness on the tree.
I am risen, I am risen from the grave,
Of my sins, my griefs, my sickness, and the waves,

"Of the resurrection life, and holy power,
Thrill my being with His new life every hour.
Now the lightnings of God's Spirit burn my soul,
Flames of His divine compassion o'er me roll,
Lightning power of God's own Spirit strikes the power of hell.
God in man, Oh Glory! Glory! All the story tell.

"I have proved Him, I have proved Him. It is true.
Christ's dominion yet remaineth, 'tis for you,
Let the fires of holy passion sweep your soul.
Let the Christ who death has conquered take control.
He will use you, He will use you. Zion yet has Saviors still,
Christ the Conqueror only waiteth for the action of your will."

Holiness Unto the Lord

This message was given in tongues and interpretation to John G. Lake in Spokane, Washington, March 6, 1916.

Holiness is the character of God. The very substance of His being and essence of His nature is purity. The purpose of God in the salvation of mankind is to produce in man a kindred holiness, a radiant purity like unto that of God Himself.

If God were unable to produce in him such a purity, then His purpose in man would be a failure, and the object of the sacrifice of Jesus Christ would be a miscarriage instead of a triumph.

The triumph of Jesus Christ was attained through His willingness to be led by the Spirit of God. The triumph of the Christian can be attained only in a similar manner. Even though God has baptized a soul with the Holy Spirit, there yet remains, as with Jesus, the present necessity of walking in humility, and permitting the Spirit of God to be his absolute guide.

The unveiling of consciousness, of the desire of the flesh, of the sensuality of the nature and the thought of man, the revelations of adverse tendencies, is part of God's purpose, and necessary for growth in God. How can the nature of man be changed except that nature is first revealed? So there arises in the heart the desire and prayer for the Spirit of God to eject, crucify, and destroy every tendency of opposition to the Holy Spirit.

Think not that thou shalt attain the highest in God until within thine own soul a heavenly longing to be like Him Who gave His life for us possesses thine heart.

Think not to come within the court of God with stain upon thy garments. Think not that heaven can smile upon a nature fouled through evil contact. Think not that Christ can dwell in temples seared by flames of hate. No! The heart of man must first be purged by holy fire and washed from every stain by cleansing blood. Know ye that he whose nature is akin to God's must ever feel the purging power of Christ within?

He who would understand the ways of God must trust the Spirit's power to guide and keep. He who would tread the paths where angels tread, himself must realize seraphic purity. Such is the nature of God. Such the working of the Spirit's power. Such the attainment of him who overcomes. In him the joy and power of God shall be. Through him the healing streams of life shall flow. To him heaven's gates are opened wide. In him the kingdom is revealed.

Fear not to place thy hand within the nail-pierced palm. Fear not to trust His guidance — the way He trod is marked by bleeding feet and with many tears. He leadeth thee aright and heaven's splendor soon shall open to thy spirit, and thou shalt know that all triumphant souls — those who have overcome indeed — have found their entrance by this path into the realm of light.

PART VII

His Message

Part VII:

His Message

Triune Salvation

John G. Lake once spoke to a conference of ministers of the Church of England which was presided over by the Bishop of London, who had this to say of his message:

"It contains the spirit of primitive Christianity and reveals the distinction between the Christian soul of the first and twentieth century, the Spirit of Christ's dominion, by which Christianity attained its spiritual supremacy. . . . It is one of the greatest sermons I have ever heard and I recommend its careful study by every priest.

"Mr. Lake had been invited to address us and has traveled 7,000 miles to be here. A committee of the Church of England was sent to South Africa to investigate Mr. Lake, his work, his person, teaching and ministry and his presence here is the result of their satisfactory report.

"Following is the text of the sermon delivered by John G. Lake in London, England, and in Washington, D.C., in December, 1913:

. . . I pray God your whole spirit and soul and body be preserved blameless [without defilement, corruption] unto the coming of our Lord Jesus Christ.

Faithful is he that calleth you, who also will do it.

1 Thessalonians 5:23,24

In the beginning of all things, even before the creation of man at all, there was a condition in which all things that existed were obedient to God. Angels were obedient to the Lord. But there came a time when angels themselves rebelled against the government of God.

In Isaiah, Satan is spoken of [as], ". . . Lucifer, son of the morning. . ." [Isaiah 14:12]. Again the Word says in substance concerning him, "Wast thou not pure and holy until pride was found in thine heart?" [Ezekiel 28:15.]

Pride was the condition which, in the angel who was pure and holy, generated the desire to be separated from God, and to rebel against Him.

It was the same pride or desire to substitute his will for the will of God which caused Adam to sin. From Adam humanity had derived the same instinctive desire to insist on their way instead of God's way; through the continued exercise of the human will and the world's way, the race has drifted into misty conceptions of the real will and the real way of God. This is particularly true in regard to the nature and substance of God.

It seems difficult to think of Him as a being and a substance. God is Spirit, but a Spirit is not a materiality. And God Himself is a materiality, a heavenly, not an earthly materiality. The forms of angels are a substance, otherwise they would not be discernible. It is not an earthly substance or material, but a heavenly one.

As we think of the substance of which heavenly beings are composed, and of which God Himself must necessarily be a composition, the mind settles on light and fire and spirit as a possibility.

Then the Word tells us that God breathed into Adam the breath of life, "and man became a living soul" [Genesis 2:7]. There came a time when God made man. The Word tells us that He made man's body of the substance of the earth. [v. 7.] He made man, the Word says, ". . .God created man in his own image, in the image of God created he him. . ." [Genesis 1:27], not just in the form that God has, but God breathed into him His own self, His own being — that heavenly materiality of which God consists. He injected or breathed Himself into the man, and the man then became a composition of that heavenly substance or materiality, and earth or the substance of earth.

Adam was the created son of God. He was just like God. He was just as pure as God was pure. God fellowshipped with him. The Word of God tells us that God came down into the garden in the cool of the day, and walked with Adam, and talked with Adam. There was perfect fellowship between God and Adam. He was a sinless man. He could look right into the face of God, and his eyes nor his spirit did not draw back. The purity of God did not startle him. He was just as pure as God was pure. That was the original man.

Man being composed of God, of heaven, of a heavenly materiality, and his body of the earth, being a sovereign like God, being on an equality with God in sinlessness, God treated him on an equality, and giving him dominion over the earth, man was a reigning sovereign on the earth. Everything, all conditions, spiritual and physical, were subject to that God-man.

The way of sin was this, that man chose to follow the inclinations of his earth-being, animal consciousness, or body, instead of his God-man, God-being, or spirit. The result was that because of the suggestion of Satan there developed calls of the earth for the earthly. After a while he partook of things earthly and became earthly himself. Therefore the fall of man was his fall into himself. He fell into his own earthly self, out of his heavenly estate, and the separation was absolute and complete.

God had said, "In the day that thou sinnest, thou shalt die." [Genesis 2:17, paraphrased.] That is, in the day thou sinnest, partaking of that which is earthly, the conditions of the earth being that of decay, the death process begins. So death reigneth from the time that sin came.

Sickness is incipient death. Death is the result of sin. There is no sickness in God. There never was, there never will be, there never can be. There was no sickness in man, in the God-man, until such time as he became the earth-man, until by the operation of will he sank into himself and became of the earth, earthly. Therefore, sin is the parent of sickness in that broad sense. Sickness is the result of sin. There could have been no sickness if there had been no sin.

Man, having fallen into that condition and being separated from God, needed a Redeemer. Redemption was a necessity because the Word says, ". . .Ye must be born again" [John 3:7]. God had to provide a means of getting man back into the original condition in which he had once been.

One man cannot save another because one man is of the earth, earthly, even as another is, and man in the natural cannot save another. One cannot elevate another into a spiritual condition or put that one in a spiritual condition which he is not in himself.

Thus it became necessary for God, in order to redeem the race, to provide a means of reuniting God and man. So Jesus was born, even as Adam had been made. He was begotten of God. He was born of God, but he partook of the tendencies of the natural life and received His natural, physical body through His mother, Mary.

The Word of God speaks of the first Adam and the last Adam. They were both Adams. They both came to produce a race. The first Adam had fallen and sinned. Therefore the race that was produced through him was a race of sinful people with the same tendencies in their natures which were in his.

The last Adam, Jesus, had no sin. He had exactly the same privilege that the first Adam had. He could have sinned if He so chose. Jesus was a man in this world, just as every man is. "For verily he took not on him the nature of angels; but he took on him the seed of Abraham" [Hebrews 2:16].

He did not take upon Him a heavenly condition, He took upon Himself the natural condition of the human family — fallen human nature.

But Jesus Christ triumphed over that condition of fallen human nature and did not sin, though the Word of God emphasizes that He was ". . . in all points tempted like as we are, yet without sin" [Hebrews 4:15]. The Word also says, "For in that he himself hath suffered being tempted, he is able to succour them that are tempted" [Hebrews 2:18]. This is what makes Him a sympathetic Savior and Christ.

The purpose of Jesus in the world was to show us the Father. So Jesus came and committed Himself publicly at His baptism at the Jordan before all the world in these words, "unto all righteousness," to do the will of God. He willed not to obey His own natural human will, but to do the will of the Father, and to be wholly and solely and entirely obedient to the will of God. He declared, ". . . I seek not mine own will, but the will of the Father which hath sent me" [John 5:30].

When a Christian is born of God, and becomes a real Christian, he is made a Christ-man, just as we who want to look upon the Father and understand Him, look upon the man Jesus, Who was the embodiment of the Father. Everything that Jesus did was the will and the word of the Father. So everything the Christian does, if he is a real one, should be the will and word of Jesus Christ.

The Christian commits himself as entirely to the will of Jesus and becomes a Christ-man as Jesus committed Himself to the will of the Father and became a God-man. . . .the secret of Christianity is not in doing. The secret is in being. Real Christianity is in being a possessor of the nature of Jesus Christ. . . .

Jesus gave us the secret of how to live this kind of life. Jesus showed us that the only way to live this life was to commit oneself, as He did, to the will of God and not walk in his own ways at all, but walk in God's ways. So the one who is going to be a Christ-man, in the best sense, and let the world see Jesus in him, must walk in all the ways of Jesus, and follow Him. He must be a Christ-man, a Christian, or Christ-one.

Therefore, the things which possess the heart and which are unlike God fasten themselves because the inner being is not subject to the will of God. One of the reasons for this low standard of Christian living is the failure to recognize the trinity of our own being. Man is triune — body and soul and spirit — just the same as God is triune, being Father and Son and Holy Ghost.

Salvation begins at the time when the spirit is surrendered to God, when the name is written in the Book of Life, and we receive the conscious knowledge of sins being forgiven. Then God witnesses to the spirit that our sins are blotted out. The Word, in the eighth [chapter] of Romans, says: "The Spirit itself beareth witness with our spirit, that we are the children of God" [Romans 8:16]. That is, the testimony of the Spirit of God to our spirit is that we are the children of God when we surrender our spirits to God.

People wonder why, after having given their hearts to God and after having received a witness of the spirit, they are troubled with evil desires and tempted to evil ways. The nature has three departments, and therefore, the surrender of the spirit to God is not all that He demands. God demands also the mind and the body.

The mind is the soul life; and it continues being of the earth, earthy, and doing earthy things until God does something to that mind, until we seek God for a new mind. It is similar to the change which occurs in the spirit; and the mind that formerly thought evil and that had wicked conceptions becomes as the mind of Christ.

The Church at large recognizes the salvation of the mind from the power of sin, and that is why many church people will say there is no such thing as sanctification.

There are Christian bodies that believe in the power of God to sanctify the mind, even as the spirit is saved. John Wesley, in defining sanctification, says that it is: "Possessing the mind of Christ, and all the mind of Christ." An individual with all the mind of Christ cannot have a thought that is not a Christ thought, no more than a spirit fully surrendered to God could have evil within it.

In later years, as the revelation by the Spirit of God has gone on, man has begun to see that there is a deeper degree of salvation than these two. He is a triune being. As he needed salvation for the mind and spirit, so he has a body which needs to be transformed by God. The whole question of physical healing, the redemption of the body, the possible translation, the resurrection, are included there.

Christ is a Savior of the whole man; of spirit, of soul, of body. When Jesus, at the Jordan, committed Himself unto all righteousness to His Father, He committed His body just as He committed His mind and just as He committed His spirit. Christians have not been taught to commit their bodies to God, and therefore they feel justified in committing them to someone else or something else, rather than to God.

Therefore, it is clear that in a whole salvation it is just as offensive to God to commit the body to the control of man, as it would be to commit the spirit to man for salvation. Salvation for the spirit can only come through Jesus, through the blood of Christ, through receiving His Spirit. Salvation from natural thoughts and ways, and the operation of the natural mind, can only come through the natural mind being transformed into the mind of Christ. Salvation for the body is found in the same manner, by committing the body now and forever to God.

No one would think of sending to any other power than God for a remedy for the spirit. There is no spirit that one could go to, unless it is the spirit of the world or the spirit of the devil;

and one goes not to either of these for the healing of the spirit or mind.

The real Christian is a separated man. He is separated forever unto God in all the departments of his life, and so his body and his soul and his spirit are forever committed to God. Therefore, from the day that he commits himself to God, his body is as absolutely in the hands of God as his spirit or his mind (soul). He can go to no other power for help or healing, except to God.

This is what gives such tremendous force to such scriptures as this: ". . .Cursed be the man that trusteth in man, and maketh flesh his arm, and whose heart departeth from the Lord" [Jeremiah 17:5]. Second Chronicles [16:12] relates that Asa, the king of Israel, ". . .in the thirty and ninth year of his reign was diseased in his feet, until the disease was exceeding great: yet in his disease he sought not to the Lord, but to the physicians," and he died. Asa had been trusting God for many years, [Who had responded to Asa's trust] by taking his little, insignificant army and delivering the great armies into his hand. But when he became diseased in his feet, he trusted not the Lord, but the physicians, and that was the offense of Asa against God.

The impression I wish to leave is this, that a hundredfold consecration to God takes the individual forever out of the hands of all but God. This absolute consecration to God, this triune salvation, is the real secret of the successful Christian life.

When one trusts any department of his being to man, he is weak in that respect, and that part of his being is not committed to God. When we trust our minds (soul) and our bodies to man, two parts are out of the hands of God, and there remains only our spirits in tune with heaven. It ought not to be so. The committing of the whole being to the will of God is the mind of God. Blessed be His name.

Such a commitment of the being to God puts one in the place where just as God supplies health to the spirit and health to the soul, he trusts God to supply health to his body. Divine healing is the removal by the power of God of the disease that has come upon the body, but divine health is to live day by day and hour by hour in touch with God, so that the life of God flows into the body, just as the life of God flows into the mind, or flows into the spirit.

The Christian, the child of God, the Christ-man, who thus commits himself to God ought not to be a subject for healing. He is a subject of continuous abiding health. And the secret of life in communion with God, the Spirit of God, is received into the being, into the soul, into the spirit.

The salvation of Jesus was a redemption of the whole man from all the power of sin, every whit — sin in the spirit, sin in the soul, sin in the body. If salvation, or redemption, is from the power of sin and every sin in our being, then the effects that sin produces in us must disappear and leave when the source is healed. Thus, instead of remaining sick, the Christian who commits his body to God becomes at once, through faith, the recipient of the life of God in his body.

Jesus gave us an example of how perfectly the Spirit of God radiates not only from the spirit, or from the mind, but from the body also. The transfiguration was a demonstration of the Spirit of God from within the man radiating out through His person, until the illumination radiated through His clothes, and

His clothes became white and glistening, and His face shone as the light. It was the radiation of God through His flesh.

In a few instances, God permitted me to see Christians thus illuminated in a measure. I am acquainted with a brother in Chicago, whose face is illuminated all the time; there is a radiation from it. His countenance is never seen in a condition of depression, or as if the pores of his flesh are closed. There is an unmistakable something that marks him as one through whom the Spirit of God radiates.

God radiated through the purified personality of Jesus so that even His very clothes became white and glistening. Christians are Christ-men, and stand in the stead of Jesus. The Word of God says to the Christian and to the Church: "Now ye are the body of Christ..." [1 Corinthians 12:27]. The accumulated company of those who know Jesus, who really have the God-life within, are the body of Christ in the world; and through that body of Christ all the ministry of Jesus is operative.

The nine gifts of the Holy Ghost are the divine equipment of God by which the Church, His body, is forever to continue to do the works of Jesus.

> For to one is given by the Spirit the word of wisdom; to another the word of knowledge by the same Spirit;
>
> To another faith by the same Spirit; to another the gifts of healing by the same Spirit;
>
> To another the working of miracles; to another prophecy; to another discerning of spirits; to another divers kinds of tongues; to another the interpretation of tongues.
>
> 1 Corinthians 12:8-10

All these gifts Jesus exercised during His earthly ministry. The people who exercise these gifts create another practical Christ, the Church which is His body, Christ being the head.

When this truth is seen, Christianity will be on a new-old basis. The illumination of God, the consciousness of our position in the world, the consciousness of our responsibility as the representatives of Christ, places upon us as Christ-men and Christ-women the burden of Christ for a lost world. Of necessity this lifts the heart and spirit into a new contact with God, and the consciousness that if a son of God, if a Christ-man to the world, then one must be worthy of his Christ. The only way to be worthy is to be in the will of Jesus.

Men have mystified the Gospel; they have philosophized the Gospel. The Gospel of Jesus is as simple as can be. As God lived in the body and operated through the man Jesus, so the man on the throne, Jesus, operates through His body, the Church, in the world. Even as Jesus Himself was the representative of God the Father, so also the Church is the representative of Christ. As Jesus yielded Himself unto all righteousness, so the Church should yield herself to do all the will of Christ.

". . . these signs shall follow them that believe. . ." [Mark 16:17] — not the preacher, or the elder, or the priest, but the believer. The believer shall speak in new tongues, the believer shall lay hands on the sick and they shall recover. The believer is the body of Christ in the world.

The Word says: "There shall be saviors in Zion." [Obadiah 1:21, paraphrase.] As Jesus took us and lifted us up to the Father, and gave Himself to sanctify and cleanse us, so the Christian takes the world and lifts it up to the Christ, to the Lamb of God Who taketh away the sin of the world.

The wonderful simplicity of the Gospel of Jesus is itself a marvel. The wonder is that men have not understood always the whole process of salvation. How was it that men mystified it? Why is it that we have not lived a better life? Because our eyes were dim and we did not see and we did not realize that God left us here in this world to demonstrate Him, even as the Father left Jesus in the world to demonstrate the Father.

The man with Christ in him, the Holy Ghost, is greater than any other power in the world. All other natural and evil powers are less than God; even Satan himself is a lesser power. Man with God in him is greater than Satan. That is the reason that God says to the believer that he shall cast out devils.

> . . . greater is he that is in you, than he that is in the world.
>
> 1 John 4:4

The Christian, therefore, is a ruler; he is in the place of dominion, the place of authority, even as Jesus was. Jesus, knowing that all power had been given unto Him, took a basin and a towel, and washed His disciples' feet. His power did not exalt Him. It made Him the humblest of all men. So the more the Christian possesses, the more of a servant he will be.

God is the great servant of the world. The One Who continually gives to men the necessity of the hour. Through His guidance and direction of the laws of the world, He provides for all the needs of mankind. He is the great servant of the world, the greatest of all servants.

Yes, Jesus, [knew] that all power had been committed to Him, and as God gave the power to Jesus, so Jesus commits through the Holy Ghost, by His own Spirit, all power to man.

I tell you, beloved, it is not necessary for people to be dominated by evil, nor by evil spirits. Instead of being dominated, Christians should exercise dominion and control other [sic] forces. Even Satan has no power over them, only as they permit him to have. Jesus taught us to close the mind, to close the heart, to close the being against all that is evil; to live with an openness to God only, so that the sunlight of God shines in, the glory radiance of God shines in, but everything that is dark is shut out.

Jesus said: "Take heed therefore how ye hear. . ." [Luke 8:18], not "what ye hear." One cannot help what he hears, but he can take heed how he hears. When it is something offensive to the Spirit and the knowledge of God, shut the doors of the nature against it, and it will not touch you. The Christian lives as God in the world, dominating sin, evil, sickness.

I would to God, He would help us to so present Jesus in the true light, that this church, and the Church that is in the world, the Christian body, would be lifted up until they would realize their privilege in Christ Jesus. Bless God, it is coming.

By the God within, we cast out or expel from the being that which is not God-like. If you find within your heart a thought of sin or selfishness, by the exercise of the Spirit of God within you, you cast that thing out as unworthy of a child of God, and you put it away from you.

Beloved, so should we do with our bodies. So must we do when sickness or the suggestion of sickness is present with us. Cast it out as evil, it is not of God. Dominate it! Put it away! It is not honoring to Jesus Christ that sickness should possess us. We do not want disease. . . .

Evil is real. The devil is real. He was a real angel. Pride changed his nature. God is real. The operation of God within the heart changes the nature until one becomes God-men. ". . .the blood of Jesus Christ. . .cleanseth us from all sin" [1 John 1:7], until we are new men in Christ Jesus, new creatures in Christ Jesus.

The power of God, the Holy Ghost, is the Spirit of dominion. It makes one not subject to the forces of the world, or the flesh, or the devil. These are under the Christian's feet. John said: "Beloved, now are we the sons of God. . ." [1 John 3:2].

Beloved, God wants us to come, to stay, and to live in that abiding place which is the Christian's estate. This is the heavenly place in Christ Jesus. This is the secret place of the Most High.

The Word of God gives us this key. It says [of the believer]: ". . .that wicked one toucheth him not" [1 John 5:18]. When the Spirit of God radiated from the man Jesus, I wonder how close it was possible for the evil spirit to come to Him? Do you not see that the Spirit of God is as destructive of evil as it is creative of good? It was impossible for the evil one to come near Him, and I feel sure Satan talked to Jesus from a safe distance.

It is the same with the Christian. It is not only in his spirit that he needs to be rid of sin, nor in his soul he is to be pure. It is God in the body that the individual needs for a well body. It is just God that he needs.

The complaint of the devil [to God] concerning Job was: "Hast not thou made an hedge about him. . .?" [Job 1:10.] He was not able to get through that hedge to touch the man. Don't you know that the radiation of the Spirit of God around the Lord Jesus was His safeguard? The artists paint a halo around the head of Jesus. They might just as well put it about His hands, feet, body, because the radiation of the Spirit of God is from all the being.

Now the Spirit of God radiates from the Christian's person because of the indwelling Holy Ghost, and makes him impregnable to any touch or contact of evil forces. He is the subjective force himself, the Spirit of God radiates from him as long as his faith in God is active.

. . . For this purpose the Son of God was manifested, that he might destroy the works of the devil.

1 John 3:8

For whatsoever is born of God overcometh the world: . . . even our faith.

Who is he that overcometh the world, but he that believeth that Jesus is the Son of God?

1 John 5:4,5

The reason people become sick is the same reason that they become sinful. They surrender to the suggestion of the thing that is evil, and it takes possession of the heart.

Sickness is just the same. There is no difference. The suggestion of oppression is presented, and [the person] becoming frightened, the disease secures a foothold. ". . . In my name shall they (the believers) cast out devils. . ." [Mark 16:17]. The believer says: "In the name of Jesus Christ, I refuse to have this thing."

For 15 years God has let me move among all manner of contagious diseases, and I have never taken one of them. The devil could not make me take them. I have prayed with smallpox patients when the pustules would burst under the touch of my hands. I have gone home to my wife and babies, and never carried contagion to them. I was in the "secret place of the Most High." Indeed, contact with diphtheria, smallpox, leprosy, and even bubonic plague, and the whole range of diseases, was in line of my daily work in connection with the work of the Apostolic Church of South Africa.

> Behold, I give unto you power to tread on serpents and scorpions, and over all the power of the enemy: and nothing shall by any means hurt you.
>
> Luke 10:19

So the prayer of the apostle comes to us with a fresh understanding:

> . . . I pray God your whole spirit and soul and body be preserved blameless unto the coming of our Lord Jesus Christ.
>
> Faithful is he that calleth you, who also will do it.
>
> 1 Thessalonians 5:23,24

Consecration Prayer

My God and Father,
In Jesus' name I come to Thee,
Take me as I am.
Make me what I ought to be —
In spirit, in soul, in body.
Give me power to do right.
If I have wronged any,
To repent, to confess —
To restore.
No matter what it costs,
Wash me in the blood of Jesus,
That I may now become Thy child, and manifest
Thee —
In a perfect spirit, a holy mind, a sickless
body.

— Amen.

A Reply to Dr. Elwood Bulgin

The following letter from Lake to Dr. Elwood Bulgin was printed in the leading daily newspaper of Spokane, Washington, in the year in which it was written.

Dr. Frank Riale, Field Secretary of the Presbyterian Board of Education, once said of this message: ". . .'Lake's reply to Bulgin,' is the clearest statement on the truth of divine healing ever written . . . a remarkable human document."

Spokane, Washington
February 28, 1920

Dr. Elwood Bulgin

Spokane, Washington

Dear Brother in Christ:

It was my privilege to be present at your meeting at the St. Paul Methodist Church at Spokane last Monday night and listen to your sermon. I was deeply impressed by the masterful manner in which you marshaled your facts, and the spirit in which they were presented to your great audience.

Your presentation of the deity of Jesus Christ, and the sharpness with which you brought the facts of the denial of the deity of Jesus by the Christian Scientists, were striking. The masterful handling of the whole subject commanded my admiration, and I believe the admiration of a great majority of your audience.

Men can speak with frankness to each other, particularly when their interests in the Kingdom of Jesus Christ are identical. You have lived, loved, and denied yourself and suffered for the cause of the Kingdom of Christ here in the earth. I, too, have loved and suffered for my fidelity to the vision of the redemption of Jesus Christ which God revealed to me.

For twenty-five years I have labored, as few men in the world have labored for so long a period, to bring before the world as far as I could the magnificent truths of the redemptive blood and life and power of the Son of God.

Your methods and my methods have been different. You, in your forceful, philosophical manner, have undertaken to destroy faith in Christian Science through opposition, ridicule, and exposure of what you believe to be its fallacies. On the other hand, I have undertaken, concerning the healing power of God and its availability for all men today, to show the world that there is no need of any man to leave any stable Christian body in order to secure the benefits of salvation and healing specifically declared by Jesus Christ Himself to be available for every man.

Jesus, in contrast with the ancient philosophers and reformers of the past and present, first gave Himself in consecration for all Christians forever. His baptism was the dedication and commitment of Himself "unto all righteousness." He undertook to reveal the righteousness of God. Note the nature of this revelation.

Having definitely committed Himself, His body, His soul, His spirit, to God forever, immediately there descended upon Him the witness to His hundred-fold consecration. The Holy Ghost came from heaven as a dove and abode upon Him, as it ever will upon every man who will meet Almighty God with the same utterances of real consecration to God, of spirit and soul and body. This reveals the demand of God upon the Christian's person and conscience, and the answer of God from heaven to this fullness of consecration.

Being thus definitely equipped, He proceeded to the wilderness for testing by Satan, to see if this consecration of body and soul and spirit would endure.

He overcame all the efforts of Satan to tempt Him in the specific departments of His life: first, the body; second, the soul; third, the spirit. He overcame through reliance on God and His Word, and came forth in the power of the Spirit. He announced the constructive platform of His life and ministry, containing the following six planks [Luke 4:18,19]:

"The Spirit of the Lord is upon me, because he hath anointed me . . .

First: "to preach the gospel to the poor;

Second: "he hath sent me to heal the brokenhearted,

Third: "to preach deliverance to the captives,

Fourth: "and recovering of sight to the blind,

Fifth: "to set at liberty them that are bruised,

Sixth: "To preach the acceptable year of the Lord."

God's acceptance year had come. No more waiting for the year of Jubilee and all its consequent blessings. God's never-ending Jubilee was at hand in Jesus Christ.

He then went throughout all Galilee teaching in their synagogues, and preaching the Gospel of the Kingdom, and healing all manner of sickness and all manner of disease among the people, and so established forever the ideal of Christian ministry for the Church of God.

Then He empowered twelve men, and ". . . sent them to preach the kingdom of God, and to heal the sick" [Luke 9:2]. Profiting by their experience, and advancing in faith and knowledge of the power of God, He ". . .appointed other seventy also. . ." [Luke 10:1]. To the seventy He said: ". . .heal the sick that are therein, and say unto them, The kingdom of God is come nigh unto you" [v. 9]. And they returned, rejoicing [and saying to Jesus] that even the devils were subject to them, ". . .through thy name" [v. 17].

Then came His wonderful entrance into death, His redemption on the cross, His resurrection from the grave, His interview with His disciples, His last commission in which, according to Mark, He established in the Church of Christ, to be born through their preaching in all the world, the very same ministry of salvation and healing that He Himself during His earthly life had practiced. That ministry contained the message of Jesus to all the world and the anointing with power from on High, just as He had received it at His baptism. Indeed He commanded them to wait in Jerusalem until "ye shall be baptized with the Holy Ghost, not many days hence." [Acts 1:4,5.]

He declared to them that certain signs should follow, saying: ". . .these signs shall follow them that believe. . ." [Mark 16:17]. Every one, every Christian soul, was thus commissioned by Jesus to heal the sick and sinful from sickness and sin [vv. 17,18]:

"In my name shall they. . .

First: "cast out devils;

Second: "they shall speak with new tongues;

Third: "They shall take up serpents;

Fourth: "and if they drink any deadly thing, it shall not hurt them;

Fifth: "they shall lay hands on the sick, and they shall recover."

The same Holy Spirit of God which flowed through Jesus Christ, the anointing that was upon Him and which flowed through His hands and into the sick, was an impartation of God so real that when the woman touched the hem of His garment, she was conscious of the instant effect of the healing in her body through it.

". . . she felt in her body that she was healed of that plague" [Mark 5:29], while Jesus Himself was likewise conscious of an outflow. He said: ". . . Somebody hath touched me: for I perceive that virtue is gone out of me" [Luke 8:46].

Divine healing is the particular phase of ministry in which the Modern Church does not measure up to the Early Church. This failure has been due to a lack of knowledge of the real nature and the real process of Christian healing.

The above incident reveals the secret of what the power was, how the power operated, by what law it was transmitted from the disciple to the one who needed the blessing.

The power was the Holy Ghost of God, both in Jesus Christ after His baptism in the Holy Ghost, and in the disciples after the baptism of the Holy Ghost came upon them on the day of Pentecost. It flowed through the hands of Jesus to the sick: it permeated the garments He wore. When the woman touched even the hem of His garment, there was sufficient of the power of God there for her need.

The disciples healed the sick by the same method. Indeed, the Apostle Paul, realizing this law, permitted the people to bring to him handkerchiefs and aprons that they might touch his body, and when they were carried to the sick, the sick were healed through the power of God in the handkerchiefs, and the demons that inhabited their persons went out of them. [Acts 19:12.]

Herein is shown the secret of the Early Church, that which explains the whole miracle-working power of the apostles and the Early Church for four hundred years. The same is evident in branches of the Modern Church. Herein is revealed the secret that has been lost. That secret is the conscious, tangible, living, incoming, abiding, outflowing Spirit of God through the disciple of Christ who has entered into blood-washed relationship and baptism in the Holy Ghost.

This is the secret that the Modern Church from the days of the Reformation onward has failed to reveal. We have, however, retained a form of godliness, "but have denied the power thereof."

When Jesus laid His hands on people, the Holy Ghost was imparted to them in healing virtue. When the disciples and early Christians likewise laid their hands on the sick, the Holy Ghost was imparted through them to the needy one. Likewise the Holy Ghost was imparted to preachers "for the work of the ministry," including healing.

Primitive Church history abounds in examples of healing in the same manner. Paul specifically enjoins Timothy to "neglect not the gift [power] that is in thee, which was given thee by prophecy, with the laying on of. . .hands. . ." [1 Timothy 4:14]. It was an impartation of the Holy Ghost to Timothy for the work of the Christian ministry.

In the whole range of Church history, we have retained the form, but have lost its power in a great degree. The pope lays his hands on the head of the cardinals, the cardinal lays his hands on the head of the bishops, the bishop lays his hands on the head of the priests, the priest lays his hands on the head of the communicants when he receives them as members of the church.

In the Protestant church in all her branches, the laying on of hands in ordination for the ministry is practiced. But in the Early Church, it was not the laying on of hands alone, but through the laying on of hands the impartation of the definite living spirit of the living God to the individual took place. Through its power in him, he was constituted a real priest, a real elder, a real preacher with grace, healing power, and faith, anointed of God from on High.

God gave the blood of Jesus to the Christian Church. God gave the power of healing to the Christian Church in the Holy Ghost, and as long as they lived under the anointing of the Holy Ghost and exercised the faith of Jesus in their hearts, the healing power of God manifested and is still manifest where this condition exists.

Christian Science exists because of the failure of the Christian Church to truly present Jesus Christ and His power through the Spirit and minister it to the world.

Robert G. Ingersoll assailed the Holy Scriptures, laughed at the Christian God, destroyed the faith of men, wrecked their hopes and left them stranded and abandoned amid the wreckage. Through this means, he brought the just condemnation of the world upon himself. The world condemns him to this hour in that he destroyed the faith of men without supplying to their souls something to take its place, as he should have done, and as any man who is honorable and true must do.

You recommended divine healing in one breath, and denied its potency in the next. You have attacked Christian Science, the followers of Dowie, and others, and arraigned them at the bar and condemned them, without giving to men a tangible way by which the healing of God might be brought to them.

Why do you not study and practice Jesus Christ's own way of healing and so make your ministry constructive? What are you going to do with the multitude of dying that the doctors cannot help? Leave them to die? The doctors have got through with them. . . . [even though], in many instances, . . . they are still prescribing for them and are perfectly aware of their inability to heal. . . [them], and are candid and willing to say so.

Dr. Bulgin, what have you got for these [medically incurable, suffering people]? What have you given to these?

If a man were walking down the street with a very poor set of crutches and a ruffian came along and kicked the crutches from under him and let him fall, every honest soul would rise in condemnation of the ruffian's act and [would] demand reparation.

You come to the dying, kick their hope from under them, and let them fall to the ground, and leave them there to die without bringing them the true healing power in the blood and spirit of Jesus. It is not sufficient to say, "I believe in divine healing." If they are sick, they must be healed.

This must not be construed as a defense of Christian Science. It is not given with that thought, nor in that spirit. It is given rather in the hope that, as an influential man in the Christian Church, you may see the weakness of your position and of the position of the Church, and by the grace of God call the Church back again to faith in Jesus Christ, the Son of God, for healing for every man from every disease, as Jesus Christ intended it should be and as the scriptures definitely, positively teach, and [to] make proper scriptural provision for a definite healing ministry.

In the hope of supplying this need of the Church, the Protestant ministers of the city of Los Angeles have agreed in formal resolution to begin the teaching and study and practice of healing. How has this come to pass, and why? They have been whipped into it by the success of Christian Science.

A recent issue of a New York daily [news]paper announces that the pastors of New York have likewise undertaken to teach the people the power of God to heal.

The Protestant Episcopal Church is endeavoring through the ministry of a layman of the Church of England from the old country, a Mr. Hickson, to educate their people in the truth of healing through the atonement of Jesus Christ, the Son of God, by the laying on of hands and the prayer of faith. In a few days, the gentleman will appear at All Saints Cathedral, Spokane, for that purpose, and the sick will be invited to be ministered to in the name of the Son of God and healed through His blood purchase.

The Church of England in England, and also in Africa, for ten years has been endeavoring to organize societies, not to teach their people Christian Science, psychic therapeutics, or mental healing, all of which belong to the realm of the natural, but to teach and demonstrate the pure power of God from heaven by the Holy Ghost, purchased by the blood of Jesus Christ, to heal diseases.

Frank N. Riale, a secretary of the Presbyterian Board of Education of New York, with sixty-three universities and colleges under his control and supervision, is the author of a remarkable book, *The Sinless, Sickless, Deathless Life,* in which he recounts in a chapter entitled, "How the Light and the Fire Fell," the marvelous story of his own conversion.

He was a minister of the Gospel and a graduate of Harvard. He found his Lord at the hands of an Indian in Dakota. He tells of the light of God that came to his soul in sanctifying power through the ministry of a Salvation Army officer, Col. Brengle. He relates his marvelous healing, when a diseased and dying wreck, through the reading of a religious tract on healing and his experience in seeing many healed of all manner of diseases by the power of God.

You are a Presbyterian, my brother. You need not go out of your own church for the truth of God concerning healing.

The question before the Church now that the break toward healing has come, and it has come, is, who is prepared to teach and demonstrate the truth of God concerning healing? Will it be a fact that in the absence of knowledge of God by the ministry of the Church, and absence of the anointing of the Holy Ghost in power upon the ministry of the Church for healing, will the Church in her blindness and ignorance and helplessness be overwhelmed by Christian Science, New Thought and the thousand and one cults which teach psychological healing?

Where is the prophet of God who should come forward, teach and demonstrate the pure spiritual value and power of the Holy Ghost, secured for men because Jesus Christ, the Son of God, gave His blood to get it for them? Is it not time that such men as yourself arise in the dignity of Christ and throw off the shackles of formal religion, and by the grace of God enter into the Holy Ghost, and rescue the Church out of her present degradation, re-establishing forever divine healing on its true and scriptural basis, the atonement of Jesus Christ?

Twenty-five years ago, the light concerning healing came to my soul, after four brothers and four sisters had died of diseases, and when four other members of the family were in a dying state, abandoned by the physicians as hopeless, and after my father had spent a fortune trying to obtain human help.

One man of God who had the truth of God in his heart came to the rescue. All four sick ones were healed.

I was an ardent Methodist. I loved my church. My parents were members of an old Scottish Presbyterian kirk [church]. The Presbyterian church had no light on the subject of healing; the Methodist church had no light on the subject of healing. I received my light through a man who had been a minister of the Congregational Church. He knew God. He knew Christ the Lord. He knew the power of God to save, and the power of God to heal.

When I accepted this blessed truth and saw my family healed out of death, what was the attitude of the church? Just what the attitude of all the leading churches has been. When I declared this truth before our conferences, she undertook to ostracize me; and from that day to this, many of her ministry, who have prayed through to God and secured the blessing and power of God upon their soul to heal the sick, have been forced out of her ministry.

Dr. Bulgin, is it not time to quit attacking forms of faith, whether good or bad, and turn your attention and the attention of the Church to the only thing that will deliver her out of her present wretchedness and inability to bless, and to bring her back again to Christ, to the foot of the cross, to the blood of Jesus, to the Holy Ghost from on High, to the power of God and the real faith, including healing, ". . .once delivered unto the saints" [Jude 3]?

Through this healing ministry, the church at Spokane reports 100,000 healings by the power of God through five years of continuous daily efforts and the kindred blessed fact that the majority of those healed were saved from sin also.

The dying world is stretching out her hands for help. The Church, on account of her laxness in this matter, opens the door for the existence of Christian Science and all the thousand and one worn-out philosophies that follow in her train. Let the manhood of the Church arise, take the place of the prophet of God, call her back to the ministry of real salvation, a blessed salvation, not alone for men after they are dead, or that will give them bliss in heaven when they die, but to a salvation that gives eternal life in Christ, health for the mind, and health for the body, and supplies likewise the power of God for the immediate need, for the need of the sick, for the need of the sinful, the wretched and dying and sin-cursed and disease-smitten.

Let the Church return in the glory of God and the power of Christ to the original faith as clearly demonstrated in the New Testament, as perpetuated forever in the Church through the nine gifts of the Holy Spirit, demonstrating beyond controversy that as long as the Holy Spirit is in the Church, so long are the gifts of the Holy Spirit not only present, but exercisable through faith.

See First Corinthians, chapter 12 [verses 8-10]:

"For to one is given by the Spirit. . ."

First: "the word of wisdom;

Second: "to another the word of knowledge. . .;

Third: "To another faith . . .;

Fourth: "to another the gifts of healing. . .;
Fifth: "To another the working of miracles;
Sixth: "to another prophecy;
Seventh: "to another discerning of spirits;
Eighth: "to another divers kinds of tongues;
Ninth: "to another the interpretation of tongues."

The unchanging order of government, spiritual enduement, and ministry of the gifts of the Spirit are further declared as follows: "And God hath set some in the church, first *apostles,* secondarily *prophets,* thirdly *teachers,* after that *miracles,* then *gifts of healings, helps, governments,* diversities of tongues" [v. 28].

When the Church exercises these gifts, then she may condemn Christian Science, Dowieism, or New Thought; then she may condemn every other philosophical cult; then she may condemn Unitarianism, and everything else that you preach against.*

Though she will not need to. Jesus never did. There were just as many strange philosophies in His day as in ours. The constructive righteousness of Christ, the presence of the living Son of God to save and heal, the revelation to the world of His divine power will stop the mouths of every "ism" and manifest one glorious, triumphant, all-embracing power of God through Jesus Christ, His Son, and its everlasting superiority.

Neither will you be compelled, as you are, to glorify doctors, medicines, surgery, etc., when the greatest physicians on earth have deplored their inability to deliver the world from its curse of sickness. Then you can not only teach the theory of the atonement of our Lord and Savior Jesus Christ, but demonstrate its reality and power to save both soul and body.

---

*Editors Note: Dowieism refers to his theology of later years.

All the abstract criticism in the world is powerless to stop the drift from the churches to Christian Science so long as Christian Science heals the sick and the Church does not. Men demand to be shown. When the authority of Jesus to forgive sins was challenged, He met the challenge with the healing of the palsied man, not with negations and criticisms. He said:

Whether is it easier to say to the sick of the palsy, Thy sins be forgiven thee; or to say, Arise, and take up thy bed, and walk?

But that ye may know. . . .

I say unto thee, Arise, and take up thy bed, and go thy way. . . .

Mark 2:9-11

He was too big for abstract criticism. So must the Christian and Church become.

Spiritualism

Editor's note: The sermon below is not printed in its entirety.

Then said Saul unto his servants, Seek me a woman that hath a familiar spirit, that I may go to her, and enquire of her. . . .

Then said the woman, Whom shall I bring up [from the dead] unto thee? And he said, Bring me up Samuel. . . .

And he said unto her, What form is he of? And she said, An old man cometh up; and he is covered with a mantle. And Saul perceived that it was Samuel. . . .

And Samuel said to Saul, Why hast thou disquieted me, to bring me up? . . . .

1 Samuel 28:7,11,14,15

The old prophet appeared [from the dead] and proceeded to tell what was going to take place and what was going to happen to Saul and his sons in the battle to come. . . .

Now then, we read a surprising thing. He had light in the promise of Christ's redemption. Where did he get it? The Word says [in] "sheol" or the regions of the dead. They [Samuel and the Old Testament saints] were there without something. What was it? The deliverance of the Son of God.

The prophets prophesied concerning the deliverance the Son of God was to bring, and after[wards] Jesus Christ entered into the regions of the dead and liberated those who were held by its chains, those who had died in the hope of the promise, those who had died in the fullness of faith that the Redeemer was to come.

He came and the actual deliverance from the power of death took place. ". . . . he led captivity captive. . ." [Ephesians 4:8]. He ascended up on High [taking with Him those who had been held in captivity], and their place of residence was transferred from that place (sheol), governed by the power of death and the angel of death, to wherever the Lord Jesus Christ went.

They ascended up on High and their place of residence was changed. We do not know where those who went with Jesus stopped. You call it Paradise, but so far as Jesus is concerned, it is perfectly plain in the Word that He never stopped until He came to the throne of God.

You go through the Book and find where anyone was ever called down out of heaven, and you won't find it. Those who have their residence with the Lord Jesus Christ, from the day of His resurrection and onward, would have to be called down, not up.

Now one of the things we have lost out of our Protestant faith from the days of the Reformation onward has been the wonderful truth of the ministry of Jesus in the Spirit to the dead. Do you get it? The ministry of Jesus to the dead.

For this cause was the gospel preached also to them that are
dead. . . .

1 Peter 4:6

"Oh, you mean dead in this world, and dead in sins?"

Not at all, because the rest of the verse explains:

For this cause was the gospel preached also to them that are
dead, . . .

Why?

. . .that they might be judged according to men in the flesh, but
live according to God in the spirit.

[They were judged] on the same grounds that men in the flesh
were. They heard the words of Jesus, [and either] they received
the words of Jesus, or [else] they rejected the words of Jesus, just
as men in the flesh do.

"Well, what does that mean?" you ask. "Are you preaching on
the subject of a second chance?"

No, brother, but I am calling attention to the state of the dead
before Jesus came. They died in the hope of the promise. Jesus
came and the promise was fulfilled. He fulfilled it on the cross
of Calvary, and went into the regions of the dead and fulfilled
it to them, and delivered them and took them out of the power
of death and transferred them to His kingdom.

. . .he led captivity captive, and gave gifts unto men.

Ephesians 4:8

With the above thoughts, I have laid a kind of foundation.
There is no such thing in the whole Old Testament as a
reoccurrence of those instances I have just read. No such a
suggestion or its possibility in the New Testament. It belonged
to a day and an age and a state that ceased to be when Jesus
Christ the Lord and Redeemer came.

[The following message in] tongues [was] given to Fred Wilson . . . [as was its] interpretation:

"Oh, listen to the Word, the Living Word of God that is coming forth. You shall live, you shall live throughout eternity; but deny the Living Word and ye shall go down, ye shall go down into the pit. Believe the Word and ye shall live."

A number of years ago, when I was a missionary in Africa, I formed the acquaintance of W. T. Stead, who later was one of the victims of the Titanic. I came to London at his invitation and expense for a personal interview. He took me to his office and, after we had become acquainted, he introduced this fact: He maintained a spiritualistic bureau associated with his great work, known as the Julia Bureau. Julia was a friend who had died, and he believed after she was dead he could contact the spirit of Julia. So eventually he published a book entitled "Letters From Julia." Later he changed the name to "After Death," and these letters from Julia are published in this book.

Stead presented me with a copy of the book and requested that I should read it carefully. I did so and made notations of the various letters, and when I got a chance to talk to him, I said:

"Julia in a very cunning manner indeed avoids the deity and divinity of the Lord Jesus Christ. Now in order that you may see it, I went over the different letters where reference was made to the Lord Jesus Christ."

I said, "You listen, Stead, that cunningness is altogether out of harmony with the other statements in the other letters of the book."

When it came to that subject of the divinity of Jesus, the peculiar cunningness of wording was observable, even to the most ordinary mind, by which she carefully, studiously avoided any reference to the divinity or deity of Jesus Christ ". . .every spirit that confesseth not that Jesus Christ is come in the flesh is not of God. . ." [1 John 4:3].*

Men come in the name of science. Naturally there is a certain reverence for knowledge, but don't you be fooled. Just because somebody comes along with the light of worldly knowledge, no matter how. . .wonderful it may seem, the knowledge he has is worldly; the knowledge you have is heavenly. The knowledge that his soul possesses is material; the knowledge that your soul possesses is divinely spiritual. It comes from the heart of the Son of God. . . .The vital things belong to the kingdom of God, to the knowledge of Jesus Christ. The vital things belong to the Holy Ghost.

It would take too long to tell of the thousands that have gone to spiritualism. I mean people honestly deceived. Just one instance.

I had a little friend, [Mr.] Jude, and his dear wife. They were old-fashioned Methodist people. They had one dear daughter who died at sixteen. I was absent most of the time in the city, but our home in the country joined theirs. Some friends said to me one night, "You know, our old friends Jude [and his wife], whose daughter died, some months past a spiritualist medium came to South Bend and they began attending [his] meetings. They have gone wild over the thing. We did not know how to help them, and wondered if you cannot help them."

---

*Editor's note: The verbatim quote is: ". . .every spirit that confesseth that Jesus Christ is come in the flesh is of God."

I went over and had a talk with them, and went {to meet the spiritualist} with them. At the proper time, this gentleman was supposed to be giving them a message from their daughter.

After they got through, I said, "I would like to talk to her," and I began to talk to this spirit. I said, "Are you Miss Jude? Where were you born? Where did you go to school?"

"The Willow Street School."

"Where did you attend church?"

"The Willow Street Methodist Church."

The answers were perfectly correct. Finally I said, "I remember a night at the Willow Creek Methodist Church when a very wonderful thing happened to you. Do you remember what that was?"

She did not know anything about it.

I said, "Your memory doesn't seem to be good. Don't you remember when a revival meeting was being conducted and you sat with Mrs. Lake and myself, and when the altar service came I invited you to go and give your heart to the Lord, and you did, and the glory of God came into your soul?"

She did not remember anything about that.

I said, "That is strange. Don't you remember on certain occasions you used to come to our home, and we used to kneel and the glory and presence of God came on your soul?"

She did not remember anything about that.

I said, "You are not the spirit of Miss Jude. You are an old liar. In the name of Jesus Christ, you get out of here."

And it got out.

Beloved, do not be fooled by every voice you hear.

One other thing, [Sir Arthur] Conan Doyle is greatly distressed about President Coolidge, and he thinks the proper thing to do is to immediately confer with the spirit of [the late] President Harding and be directed about the things of state, or he will make some blunder. This is the advice of one of the greatest scientists of all the world, a man who has been knighted by the King of England because of his knowledge of scientific methods. Strange council, a darkened soul. Bright mind filled with knowledge of this world, but a darkened soul without a knowledge of eternal things. Do you see the distinction?

The instance I told you of has been the practice of men whenever they have had opportunity to go into such matters. One of these days, the first time I hear somebody announcing that they are going to confer with President Harding, I am going to present myself. In case of a public man, his speeches are on record, and they have been available to everybody.

Here is an example. In Edenburgh, I attended a seance where the medium was giving a wonderful message, supposedly from the spirit of the late W. E. Gladstone [British statesman and four-time Prime Minister]. I put in my pocket several copies of Gladstone's addresses. I had a stenographer take down the message, and I took the old addresses I had in my pocket and this one that had come through the medium and compared them.

I said, "It seems to me that something terrible has happened to W. E. Gladstone if he is the author of this message. The thing isn't comparable with the things he uttered in this life. It looks to me as if dying has had an awful bad effect on him."

They were very much surprised. Most mediums have gotten wise now. Comparison is a wonderful thing.

There is one source of knowledge; that is God. The sin of spiritualism is in this fact: God said to His ancient people Israel, "Thou shalt not seek unto them that peep and mutter." [Isaiah 8:19a.] This describes the conditions prevalent in any seance.

What should they do? ". . . should not a people seek unto their God?. . ." [Isaiah 8:19b]. This word of God does not even give me the privilege of seeking guidance of angels, let alone the spirit[s] of the dead, or the spirit of a living man either. It gives me one privilege. There is One Mind that knows all, that is the mind of God, and if I am His child, and if my heart is made pure by the blood of His Son, then I have a right to come into His presence and secure anything [according to God's Word] my heart may want.

I do not believe the world has ever begun to conceive of the treasures of the wisdom of the heart of God. Our conception of the possibility of receiving wisdom and knowledge from God is very limited. Here is an experience from my own life.

In the course of my preaching in Africa, I observed [that] I would begin to quote things from the historical records that I had never heard. I could not understand it. After a while I became troubled about it and [thought that] I must stop the practice. It was going on the record as a part of my sermon, and I felt [that] if you quoted something historical, you ought to be able to lay your hand on the record in order to be convinced. Then I observed there was a difficulty when I checked these utterances.

Then I told my stenographer that when these unusual things would come, I would raise my finger and she was to put a special mark on these paragraphs. After a while I had quite a collection of them.

When I came to the United States, I had them with me. I was visiting in the office of Senator Chamberlain, talking with his secretary, Grant. As I sat talking with Grant, I showed him this list and told him my experience.

He was a Holy-Ghost-baptized man. He said, "That is an easy matter. We have the most phenomenal man in the Congressional Library here. You give him a quotation from any book, and he will tell you where to find it."

We sent the list into him one evening and left it with him overnight. The next day when we returned, he told us just where we could find each of these quotations.

Beloved, who knows the facts? Some wondering mind somewhere? Some mind of a dead man? No sir, they were in the mind of God, and the soul that enters into the mind of God can get them any time. But, beloved, it is the blood of Jesus Christ that enters there. "In whom are hid all the treasures of wisdom and knowledge" [Colossians 2:3].

Oh God, some day may we become big enough to know God, to appreciate our Christ and our Savior and the wonder of His soul and the Christian privilege of entering there.

Reign as Kings

I want to bring you a message that came to me today. I have been for years on the verge of this message, but never did I receive it until this morning.

In the fifth (chapter) of Romans and the seventeenth verse, in another translation, there is a remarkable rendering:

> For if by the trespass of the one, death reigned as king through the one, much more shall they who receive the abundance of grace

That means that the moment you accept Jesus Christ, God becomes your righteousness. That is "the gift of righteousness."

. . . It means [that] every one of us that have been born again come into a kingly and queenly state and we are accepted by God to reign as kings and queens in the realm of life. [In the past] we have reigned as servants in the realm of spiritual death. [Now] we have passed out of death, Satan's realm, into the realm of life, into the realm of the supernatural, or the spiritual, or the heavenlies.

Here are some significant facts. Man was never made a slave. He was never made for slavery. He was made to reign as king under God. If you noticed, I showed you this, that the kingly being. . .was created in the image and likeness of God, that he was created on terms of equality with God [so] that he could stand in the presence of God without any consciousness of inferiority.

I quote you from the eighth Psalm in which this expression is used:

What is man, that thou art mindful of him? and the son of man, that thou visitest him?

For thou hast made him a little lower than the angels, and hast crowned him with glory and honour.[2]

Psalm 8:4,5

---

[2]In Psalm 8:5 the word *angels* is a translation of the Hebrew word *elohiym,* and is the name of God in the first five chapters of Genesis.

What does it mean? It means that God has made us as near like Himself as it is possible for God to make a being. He made you in His image. He made you in His likeness. He made you the same class of being that He is Himself.

He made Adam with an intellect, with such caliber that he was able to name every animal, every vegetable, and every fruit, and give them names that would fit and describe their characteristics. When God could do that with man, then that man belonged to the realm of God.

Adam had such vitality in his body that even after he sinned and became mortal, he lived nearly a thousand years — 930 years — before mortality got in its work and put him on his death bed. Methuselah lived 969 years. Life was so abundant, so tremendous in their minds and spirits that it conquered century after century.

Jesus said: ". . . I am come that they might have life, and that they might have it more abundantly" [John 10:10].

More abundantly! Jesus made the declaration: "I am come that ye might have life."

The thing that was forfeited in the garden was regained. God gave him [man] dominion over the works of His hand. God made him His understudy, His king, to rule over everything that had life. Man was master. Man lived in the realm of God. He lived on terms of equality with God.

God was a faith God. All God had to do was to believe that the sun was, and the sun was. All God had to do was to believe that the planets would be, and they were. Man belonged to God's class of being — a faith man. And he lived in the creative realm of God.

JOHN G. LAKE: A MAN WITHOUT COMPROMISE

Friends, if you believe what I am preaching, it is going to end your impotence and weakness and you will swing out into a power such as you have never known in your life.

Man lost his place by high treason against God. He lost his dominion in the fall. With the fall went his dominion over spirit and soul. But universal man ever yearned for the return of his dominion.

Brother, do you hear me? Here is one of the most tremendous facts that we have to face, that never [has] a single primitive people. . . been found that has not yearned for dominion. Not a single primitive people has ever been found that did not have a Golden Past where they had dominion, a Golden Future where dominion was going to be restored. That is the tradition of universal man.

Man has craved dominion. Man has shrunk from bondage. Man has rebelled against it. Man has yearned to gain the mastery again over physical loss, over mind loss, and over the loss of spirit. This long-ago desire to gain the lost dominion is seen in his offerings, in his drinking blood, in his priesthood that he has appointed.

I want to enter this a little bit with you. Darwin foolishly said that the reason man drank blood was because the blood was salty and he craved salt.

Friends, human blood was never desirable to any people. Why did they drink it? They drank it in order that they might be like God. They drank it that they might become eternal, immortal.

The desire for immortality of the physical body lies latent in the heart of universal man. And for that reason they drank it, believing if they drank it, they would be like God. They took the animal (or man), and they laid it upon the altar of their god or gods, and when they did, they believed that the offering became identified with their god. Then they said, "If we drink the blood of the man or animal, we drink the blood of God, and if we drink enough if it, we will be God."

How far is that removed from the communion table? Do you see the analogy? The communion table is practically unknown as yet to the majority of Christians.

Now the ancients believed this, and the people of Africa, and it caused them to become cannibals. It was not because they loved human blood, but they believed if they could eat the flesh and drink the blood that was given to their god, they would be like God. You will find that all through the legends and poetry of the old world.

Universal man feels [that] the lost dominion can be regained. They have a conviction that it is going to be regained. And this faith of universal man, reaching Godward, finally challenged God to make it a possibility. He [man] believes that union with God will give him this dominion. He hates defeat. He wants to conquer death. He dreams of immortality. He fears death and disease.

Let me recapitulate. This universal man has believed that somewhere God was going to give him this lost dominion. He believed that dominion would come through his union with God, if that union could be effected. Can you understand now? It was the universal knowledge and the universal need and the universal cry of man for union with Deity that caused the Incarnation.

Let me come a step closer. On the ground of what Jesus Christ did, the substitutionary sacrifice, God is able to redeem us from our sins. He is able to impart to us His very nature. He is able

JOHN G. LAKE: A MAN WITHOUT COMPROMISE

to give us eternal life, take us into His own family, so that we can call Him "Father." Not by adoption only, but by an actual birth of our spirit, so we come into actual relationship and union with God and the age-old cry of universal man has been fulfilled.

Do you see? The New Birth has brought us into vital union with Jesus Christ.

This thing I am teaching you about your union with God is not known in the great body of Christians. All they have is forgiveness of sin. There is no actual union with God. They do not know that the New Birth is a real incarnation. They do not know that they are as much the sons and daughters of God Almighty as Jesus is. The great body of the Christian Church has no dominion, does not know it. They have the most befogged concept of what God has done and what God is to them and what they are to God.

Another step. The incarnation that God has given through the New Birth has bestowed upon us the lost authority of the Garden of Eden. And only here and there has a man known it or preached it or dared to assume it.

. . . .J. Hudson Taylor, after his first visit to China, was walking in England and a voice said, "If you will walk with Me, we will evangelize inland China." He looked, and there was no one there. An unseen angel had spoken to him. Then his heart caught the vision and said, "Lord, we will do it." He was the founder of the great China Inland Mission.

Taylor was returning on a sailing vessel and they were going through the Yellow Sea. It was in the section where the seven winds come at eventide, but from a certain hour in the day until evening there is no wind.

One afternoon the captain said to Mr. Taylor, "Take this." And he took the glasses and looked. He could see they were nearing land. The captain said, "The worst pirates in all this awful section of the ocean are there. Our vessel will strike the rocks and there is no hope of saving it."

J. Hudson said, "Are you a Christian?"

He said, "I am."

Taylor asked, "Are there any other Christians here?" He said, "Yes, the cook and carpenter and another man are Christians."

Taylor said, "Call them, and let's go pray."

He called them and the five or six of them went to their respective places. They had not been praying but a little while when he heard commands being given on board and men rushing about. He came up, and he could see the wind breaking on the sea that had been so glassy. In a few minutes the wind had filled the sails, three hours before nature would have sent it.

In my own experience, I have seen God many times set aside natural law. I told you one day about one miracle. We were putting on a roof on one of our buildings. A storm came up. The boys had unwisely torn off too many shingles for us to cover before the storm reached us.

I saw that storm go around us and leave ten or fifteen acres where the rain did not fall for more than one-half hour, and the water flowed down the gutters past our buildings. Those boys worked and sang and shouted. When the last shingle was in place, the water fell on it, and we were drenched to the skin.

I have seen God perform His prodigies in answer to believing prayer. What God does for one, He can do for another.

This inferiority complex that makes men seek God and create religions and priesthoods is a relic of the fall and comes because man is conscious that once somewhere he had power, he had dominion, and he galls under it. Like a mighty athlete who feels his strength leaving him, until by and by he becomes helpless as a little child. Oh, the agony of the thing!

Every man has within him the entire history of every man. That cry of agony of the athlete, that cry of agony of the man that once had physical and mental health is the cry of universal man, crying for the lost authority and dominion that he once enjoyed.

He seeks through rites a new birth, a re-creation that does not come. How many lodges and secret societies have a rite, a symbol of the New Birth? I cannot mention them, but you look back. You are initiated into such and such an organization. I can name four that have a new-birth rite. It is latent in the universal man.

Every religion has some kind of re-creation. Why? Every man has a consciousness (I am speaking of men who think) down in them. There is something that cries out against death, against sickness, against sorrow, against defeat, against failure. There is something that rebels against the bondage of fear and that cries for rebirth, a re-creation that will give them dominion and mastery over the forces that have held them in bondage.

Our redemption is God's answer to this universal hunger. We saw God's hunger creating man: now you see man's hunger bringing God to re-create him. Can't you understand it, men, that the hunger in the heart of God drove Him, forced Him, until He spoke a world into being for the home of His love project, man? It has driven Him to create universes to hold this world by the law of attraction and make it a safe place for man.

Then when man fell and lost his standing and became a slave and subject to Satan, then this universal cry went up until the very heart of God bled for this broken human. Then He made provision whereby this man that He had created, and [who] had sinned and [that He] had re-created, might come back into fellowship with Him of a higher, holier sort than he had lost at the beginning.

I want to take you through some scriptures. Go with me to Romans 5:17:

> For if by the trespass of one, death reigned as king through the one, much more shall they who receive the abundance of grace and the gift of righteousness, reign as kings in the realm of life, through Jesus Christ.

By the New Birth, you have passed out of Satan's dominion and Satan's power and you have come over into God's dominion, and you have come over into the kingdom of the Son of His love.

You will pardon me, but I have this consciousness when I am preaching: there comes up a wave from the congregation of a kind of stultified unbelief. Do you know where it comes from? It comes from all the years you have sat under false teachers. You have been taught that to be humble you have got to say you are a sinner, you are no good, you don't amount to anything. You sing:

"Weak and sickly,

Vile and full of sin I am."

I do not like to preach one thing, and Charles Wesley another. If you are born again, you are a son of God. And for you to tear yourself out of your sonship, your relationship and the righteousness of God, and put yourself over in the realm of death, and tell God you are dirty and unclean, that His blood has not cleansed you, and His life has not been delivered you, it is a monstrous thing. It is all right to sing that as an unregenerate, but it is not the experience of the sons and daughters of God.

Here is our position through Jesus Christ. God has become our righteousness. We have become His very sons and daughters, and you sing weakness, and you talk weakness, and you pray weakness, and you sing unbelief, and you pray and talk it, and you go out and live it.

You are like that good old woman. She said, "I do love that doctrine of falling from grace, and I practice it all the time."

Another man said, "Brother, I believe in the dual nature. I believe that when I would do good, evil is always present with me, and I thank God that evil is always there."

You live it and believe it, and God cannot do anything with you. You magnify failure and you deify failure until to the majority of you the devil is bigger than God. And you are more afraid of the devil than you are of God. You have more reverence for the devil than you do for God.

It is absolutely true. If any saint would dare to say, "I am done with disease and sickness; I will never be sick again," ninety percent of you would say, "Keep your eyes on that person. He will be sick in a week. The devil will sure get him."

You believe the devil is bigger than God. Your god is about one and a half inches high and the devil is one and a half feet high. What you need to do is to change gods and change gods quick. There have been only a few folks that had a good-sized God.

You go over in Genesis and you see the size of God. It is a full-sized photograph. You see Jesus Christ rising from the dead, and you have seen the God-sized photograph of redemption. We "reign as kings in the realm of life."

And what is the reaction in you? You say, "That is all right and I wish that was true in my case. I would like to reign as king." And you think this moment how you are whipped, and you think how you have been defeated, and how weak you are, and you will be defeated all the next week. You reckon on the strength of the devil, and on your own sickness. You say, "If he had what I have, he wouldn't talk like that."

How can the power of God come through such a mess of unbelief? How can God get near? Ninety percent of those who have received the Spirit have made God a little bit of a side issue, a sort of court of last resort.

When you get where the devil can do no more, you say: "God, catch me. The devil has finished his work." God is simply a life insurance company that pays the premium at death.

Turn with me to Ephesians 1:7:

> In whom we have redemption through his blood, the forgiveness of sins, according to the riches of his grace.
>
> Ephesians 1:7

For months and months that scripture has been burning its way into my soul. "In whom we have redemption through his blood, the forgiveness of sins...," and it is "...according to the riches of his grace."

It is illustrated in Israel coming out of Egypt, with the Red Sea before them, with [a] vast desert stretching its burning waste between them and their promised land. We do not have any such redemption in our religion. I'll tell you what we need.

Have you been in Canada? Do you know when I went to Canada for the first time, there was one thing that struck me peculiarly. The sign would read, "John Brown, Limited" [U.S. "incorporated"]. Everywhere I saw that sign. That is a Scotchman's caution.

I was holding meetings in the old St. Andrew's Church in Sidney [Australia]. I asked them one night why they did not put their national symbol on their churches. They wondered what I meant. I said, "Every other business house is Ltd. Why don't you put it over the church?"

And old Scotchman said, "We don't have to. Everybody knows it."

Limited? Sure, it is limited. Limit God, limit ourselves, limit His grace, limit the Word. Sure, our God is a little bit of a god. Most of us would carry Him in our vest pocket, and it wouldn't bulge the pocket. Our God with the Ltd. [sign] on Him.

Brother, sister, that challenge comes to us today to let God loose. There are a few places where they have let God have His way, and how the blessings have come.

"In whom we have redemption...."

Have you? If you have your redemption, it means that to you Satan has been defeated. Jesus conquered the devil as a Jew before He died. Then He let the devil conquer Him on the cross and send Him down to the place of suffering with our burden and guilt upon Him. But after He satisfied the claims of justice, Jesus met the devil in his own throne room and He stripped him of his authority and dominion. And when He arose, He said:

> I am he that liveth, and was dead; and, behold, I am alive for evermore, Amen; and have the keys of hell and of death.
>
> Revelation 1:18

He had gone into the throne room, taken Satan's badge of dominion and authority that Adam had given him in the Garden of Eden. And every man that accepts Jesus Christ was identified with Him when He did it. He did it for you. He did it for me. He died as our substitute and representative. When He put His heel on Satan's neck, He did it for you, and you are in Christ. And to you who believe, Satan is conquered and Satan is defeated. Satan can holler and bellow as much as he wants to, but you withstand him in the faith of Jesus Christ.

I saw a picture this morning. I was reading an article. I saw a company of men walk out, and I saw all the diseases and all the crimes and agonies; I saw cancers and tumors and tuberculosis; and I saw a company of men and women walk down in the midst of it, and I heard them say, "Here come the sons of God; here come the conquerors."

And the sons of God said to disease, "In the name of Jesus, depart," and disease fled. It fled as it did before the Son of God. It obeyed because the Son of God sent them out and gave them His name as authority. I saw the company of men enter into the lost dominion. They put upon them the garments of their authority and masters. They were rulers.

Then I saw another picture. I saw David in the old cave of Adullam. I saw men coming down that were broken and in distress and in debt, and men that were in awful physical conditions. And they gathered, four hundred strong, around David. And out of that crowd David developed and trained the most invincible army that was ever seen.

Then my mind passed over a few years of struggle. And I saw from that company some mighty men come forth. I saw one man come forth and go where there were thousands and thousands of Philistines; men that were shoulder above him; men that wore shields. I saw that man go among those giants and he slew thousands of them. And I piled them in hundreds until I had piled eight hundred.

Every one of those mighty men of David were simple men of extraordinary ability. There was no mark to indicate that they were more than common Jews, 5' 11", but they knocked down men 6' 6" and 6' 8". They conquered them because they were blood-covenant men.

That is the type of the Church of Jesus Christ. And I said, "Where are God's mighty men today?"

Then I saw a picture. David sat there a little way from the spring of Bethlehem, and the Philistines had gotten control of the water. David said, "Oh, that I had a drink." And those three men came forth.

He said, "Where are you going, boys?" They just waved him off, and those three men conquered the whole company of the Philistines, filled their pitchers with water, and set them down at David's feet.

I cried, "My God, my God, where are the mighty men of valor of today, the men that can assail the forces of Satan?"

God says they are coming out of you: they are going to arrive. God has in training some men and women that are going to do exploits for Him. Will you not come up and live in your realm?

This is the trouble with most of us. We live up in the faith realm, but we have gone down the back stairs into the reason realm, and a lot of you are hugging your old devilish reason right now.

God help you, brother, this afternoon to throw your reason out that had led you into all kinds of doubt and fear, to throw it to the wind and say, "God, here goes. We trust in Your omnipotence to put it over."

Additional copies of
John G. Lake: A Man Without Compromise
are available from your local bookstore,
or by writing:

HARRISON HOUSE
P. O. Box 35035
Tulsa, OK 74153

Wilford Reidt was converted to Christ at age sixteen in the fall of 1925. He spent the next eight years ministering in street evangelism throughout the western and southern United States.

In 1931 Rev. Reidt came to Spokane and to the life-changing influence of Dr. John G. Lake's powerful ministry. In 1941 Lake's daughter, Gertrude, became Wilford's wife. Together, they preserved much of Lake's teachings in their own lives and ministry as well as in a treasure of written materials.

After serving three years with the U.S. army during World War II, Mr. Reidt earned his master's degree from Whitworth College in Spokane. For the next twenty-two years he was a public school teacher while remaining active in church affairs. But above that, he was a public school teacher in the body of Christ. He was an ordained minister and president of the Ministerial Fellowship of the U.S., Inc. He published a paper for that fellowship called *His Tribune.*